Arizona
Trout Streams
and Their Hatches

Fly-Fishing in the High Deserts of
Arizona and Western New Mexico

Charles R. Meck *&* John Rohmer

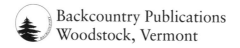

Backcountry Publications
Woodstock, Vermont

With time, access points may change, and road numbers, signs, and landmarks referred to in this book may be altered. If you find that such changes have occurred near the streams described in this book, please let the author and publisher know, so that corrections may be made in future editions. Other comments and suggestions are also welcome. Address all correspondence to:

Fishing Editor
Backcountry Publications
PO Box 748
Woodstock, VT 05091

Library of Congress Cataloging-in-Publication Data
Meck, Charles R.
  Arizona trout streams and their hatches : fly-fishing in the high deserts of Arizona and Western New Mexico / Charles R. Meck and John Rohmer
      p.   cm.
  ISBN 0-88150-423-8 (alk. paper)
  1. Trout fishing—Arizona—Guidebooks. 2. Trout fishing—New Mexico—Guidebooks. 3. Fly fishing—Arizona—Guidebooks. 4. Fly fishing—New Mexico—Guidebooks. 5. Arizona—Guidebooks. 6. New Mexico—Guidebooks. I. Rohmer, John. II. Title.
SH688.U6M423 1998
799.1'757'09791—dc21   98-29660
                                                                 CIP

Cover photo by Charles Meck; interior photographs by the authors and Ron Dungan
Maps by Paul Woodward, © 1998 The Countryman Press
Text design by Rachael Kahn
Mayfly drawing by Terry Hiner

Published by Backcountry Publications
A division of The Countryman Press
PO Box 748, Woodstock, VT 05091

Distributed by W. W. Norton & Company, Inc.
500 Fifth Avenue, New York, NY 10110

Printed in the United States of America
10 9 8 7 6 5 4 3 2 1

DEDICATION

To my wife, Shirley, and my children, Lynne and Bryan,
and my grandchildren, Lauren and Matthew.
Thanks for your encouragement.

—C.M.

I'd like to dedicate this book to my father, who taught me to
love and respect the outdoors, and who passed away last year;
and to my wife, Linda. Without her patience and perseverance,
this book would never have been completed.

—J.R.

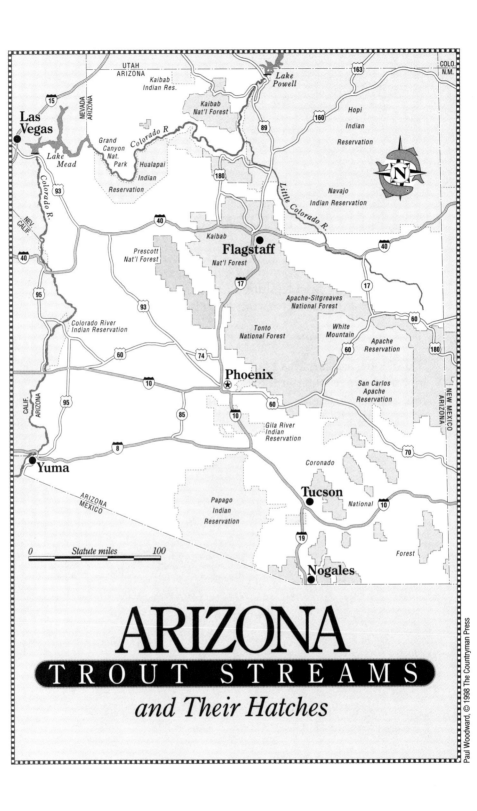

ARIZONA
TROUT STREAMS
and Their Hatches

Contents

ACKNOWLEDGMENTS

With any guidebook, a lot of people must cooperate to make it a success, and we've had many people help us with *Arizona Trout Streams*. This cooperation has ranged from information to companionship; from knowledgeable anglers to government agencies. Without their help this book could never have been completed.

Thanks to Dorothea Meck, who kept temperature records of towns and cities throughout the state used for comparison purposes in chapter 1.

Thanks to Arizona Game and Fish officials like Rich Beaudry, Information Branch chief (recently retired); Mike Weisser of the Tonto Creek Hatchery; Jim Novy, fisheries program manager in Pinetop; Bill Persons; and Michael Lopez. These men are representative of the many dedicated people within this organization.

Some of the chambers of commerce and tourist associations in Arizona helped tremendously—Pete Sesow of the Cottonwood Chamber of Commerce, in particular. Thanks also to the Happy Jack Lodge (520-477-2805) in Happy Jack; the Best Western Cottonwood Inn (520-634-5575) and Tal-wi-wi Lodge (520-339-4319) in Alpine; and Reed's Motor Lodge (520-333-4323) in Springerville. These motels and resorts went out of the way to accommodate us. They deserve your patronage. Mike Druse and Katie Shinor of Tal-wi-wi Lodge and Roxanne Knight of Reed's Motor Lodge even set up meetings with local anglers for us.

Thanks to Bob David, US Fish and Wildlife, for his help with the White Mountain Apache streams; to Brad Duncan of the Canyon Creek Hatchery; Rick Law of Big Lake Bait and Tackle; and to Dave Foster of the Marble Canyon Guide Service at Lee's Ferry. Kelly Meyer, fisheries biologist for the White Mountain Apache Tribe, also gave us a lot of information on the streams and rivers there.

Rick Thomas showed us Oak Creek and some of its hatches. Bob Tulk gave us information on many of the Alpine-area streams.

Patti Spindler, aquatic ecologist of the Arizona Department of Environmental Quality, helped tremendously with the hatches of Arizona. Indeed, it would have been impossible for us to create a hatch chart on each stream without this organization's help.

1

Introduction

What comes to your mind when someone mentions Arizona—deserts, dryness, hot weather? Or maybe you'd think of saguaro cacti, rattlesnakes, scorpions, and Gila monsters. And of course you'd be right.

But how about ponderosa pines? Arizona actually has the largest stand of ponderosa in the United States. And there's more that might amaze you: Fly-fishing over trout rising to a hatch; catching native Apache trout in a cool meadow in midsummer; streams very near Phoenix on which you can fly-fish a hatch every day of the year. These are what I think of when I think of Arizona. The state boasts over 160 cold streams and rivers and more than 40 productive lakes—many of them located in heavy stands of pines. In addition to scenery and trout, you'll find some respectable hatches on these waters.

A friend and fellow angler, Craig Josephson invited me on a trip to Arizona about 5 years ago. I had serious doubts about fly-fishing in this desert state. I hadn't heard much about the angling here, except for the Colorado River and Lee's Ferry. That one area had plenty of publicity. But we were planning to fly-fish far from the Colorado—in the White Mountains, 200 miles east-northeast of Phoenix. Craig planned the trip for late May. I met him in the Valley of the Sun, still apprehensive, and we took the four-hour trip to the Pinetop-Lakeside area. We arrived at Sunrise Lake, about 9000 feet above sea level, early on Sunday morning. Craig had arranged for Bob and Josh David to meet us there and fish with us—in float tubes, no less, another first for me.

I started with a Peacock Lady pattern. I landed dozens of rainbows and Apache trout! Then, about 10 AM, I met my first Arizona hatch on

Sunrise Lake. Speckle-winged duns appeared on the surface, and trout fed sporadically on them. All of us switched to a size 16 Adams and caught still more trout on the surface.

Sunrise Lake was the beginning of a successful and memorable trip to Arizona. That week we fly-fished the Little Colorado River, the North and East Forks of the White River, and several small streams, all loaded with native Apache trout.

It didn't take me long to find out that the Salt River, just a few miles out-side of Phoenix, held trout all year long. The Verde River, also in the Val-ley of the Sun, likewise hosts trout in winter. Just think—fly-fishing all winter long in temperatures between 60 and 75 degrees in a desert set-ting. That week in the White Mountains really changed my thinking on Arizona trout fishing.

So when the next winter in Pennsylvania grew severe, my wife and I headed to Arizona. Now that I knew I could fish here, I was ready for the move. Arizona residents call the likes of us snowbirds. I don't agree; I think the real snowbirds are those who come to the Valley of the Sun but don't take an active role in the area's activities or mingle with the locals. I take a different approach. In my first trip to the area I presented a couple of talks to the Desert Flyfishers and Arizona Flyfishers organizations, in Mesa and Phoenix respectively, and fly-fished with many of their members.

Shortly after I arrived in Arizona that December a few years ago, I started learning about its waters. Many of Arizona's trout streams empty into three major rivers, two of which end up near Phoenix: The Salt River flows from the northeast out of the White Mountains, where it picks up flow from the Black and White Rivers; Oak, Beaver, and West Clear Creeks, along with the East Verde River, empty into the Verde River in the Cottonwood area. The Verde joins the Salt River at the Phon D. Sutton recreation area, just 15 miles east of Phoenix. East Clear and Chevelon Creeks flow north on the Mogollon Rim and empty into the Little Col-orado, Arizona's third major river. The Little Colorado empties into the Colorado near the Grand Canyon.

Not only do Arizona rivers hold trout, but they also offer a good num-ber of hatches. Have you ever heard of seeing tricos in February? I've seen tricos on the Salt River throughout the winter months. Travel to the upper Verde River in Cottonwood, 90 miles north of Phoenix, and you'll encounter trico hatches from late February throughout spring. The Salt also holds a great little blue-winged olive dun hatch; I've fished this spin-ner fall many evenings in January and February. And you'll see other great hatches—green drakes, blue quills, and pale evening duns—on many of the state's waters. In February and March a year ago I fly-fished on seven different Arizona trout streams. All seven hosted a great little black stonefly hatch in midafternoon. Caddis hatches abound on Arizona streams, too; I've hit green caddis hatches that brought trout to the surface in February on the upper Verde. The same hatches occur on the Salt in late March.

THE DOWNSIDE

Arizona trout fishing has its problems, too. Just about every drop of water that flows in the Verde and Salt Rivers ends up ignominiously in canals that line the Phoenix landscape. Because water is so precious in this desert, the two rivers serving the area suffer. On many winter days I've seen only a trickle of water in the Salt River below Saguaro Lake. In November and December the Salt River Project (SRP) often limits the flow to 8 cubic feet per second. In 1997 the flow was restricted to that anemic level in January and February also; in 1998 the SRP limited the flow all the way into April. The Arizona Game and Fish Department receives no prior information about when SRP plans to lower the water. I've seen numerous occasions when the state stocked the Salt just below the dam—and the next day the SRP lowered the water flow. When this occurs you can see hundreds of trout swimming in the shallow water, trying to feed. The dozens of blue herons along the Salt look forward to these days; anglers don't. If only the SRP would cooperate with the Game and Fish Department, we would all benefit.

Many of the trout streams in Arizona warm considerably in summer. The state stocks the upper Verde during the late-fall and winter months. By the time May arrives, however, this and many other streams have risen above comfortable temperature levels for trout. This rise is inevitable; look at the temperatures in the state's desert areas in late spring, summer, and early fall (see Table 1). In 1996, for instance, Mesa recorded 129 days with air temperatures of over 100 degrees.

Precipitation in the state can be meager. If snows don't come to the high country in winter, the trout streams suffer. If thunderstorms don't arrive in summer, parts of many of the smaller streams in the state run dry. And in recent years, rainfall has not been kind to Arizona trout streams. The summer of 1996 was especially cruel. The East Verde River, for example, depends on water from the Blue Ridge Reservoir; during summer 1996 parts of this river went dry. When precipitation is this low, the cold-water fisheries suffer tremendously.

Still, when precipitation does come, it can be equally damaging—and dangerous. Summer thunderstorms can be severe, with plenty of hail. The "monsoon season" here is July and August.

The small number of large trout streams in Arizona is another draw-back. Larger streams like the Verde and Salt Rivers warm considerably and are more a home for bass than trout. Most trout streams here average 10 to 25 feet in width, with very few exceptions. (The North Fork of the White River is one of those few exceptions; its status as a larger trout stream can be attributed to snowmelt from the White Mountains and the elevation at which it flows.)

Increasing population poses another problem. In 1997 Maricopa County's population grew by over 80,000 people—which makes it the fastest-growing county in the nation. And residents leave the Phoenix metropolitan area by the thousands to escape summer's intense heat. Where do all of these people go? You got it—many camp, fish, or just wade in one of the state's cooler streams. Especially on weekends you'll encounter heavy angling pressure on many of these streams. If you can, then, fish these crowded waters during the week.

TEMPERATURES

Still, Arizona is a land of diversity. Even when temperatures in and around Phoenix are unbearable, temperatures around Greer and other locations in the White Mountains are comfortable. And the cooler temperatures in Flagstaff, Sedona, Payson, and Pinetop sustain this state's trout fishing. While temperatures in the Phoenix area (at 1200 feet) may rise above 100 degrees, temperatures in Greer, at 9000 feet above sea level, might be only in the high 70s or low 80s. Why such variation? The Mogollon Rim. This escarpment rises several thousand feet above the desert floor and runs roughly from southeast to northwest, cutting the state in half just 100 or so miles north of Phoenix. The Rim marks the southern edge of the Colorado Plateau and in places rises spectacularly for as much as 2000 feet. This Rim, along with several high mountain ranges like the White, holds a good cover of snow into late spring, assuring adequate water flow throughout summer. Indeed, some of the White Mountains' peaks rise above 11,000 feet, and elevations at or near the Mogollon Rim average more than 7000. I've waded into knee-deep snowdrifts near Greer as late as mid-June, and I've encountered water temperatures at that time of year on the upper Little Colorado in the high 40s and low 50s. I've also seen my share of roads closed by snowdrifts in mid- and late-April along the Mogollon Rim. So in short, weather is variable in this state of highly varied terrain, and it is best to be prepared for anything.

Take a look at the following chart, which shows air temperatures around the state in the summer of 1997:

Table 1. Air Temperatures for Various Cities in Arizona

	PHOENIX	COTTONWOOD	PAYSON	PINETOP	FLAGSTAFF
June 1	106	102	91	85	75
June 18	104	100	91	83	80
July 1	105	103	98	89	84
July 18	110	105	99	86	87
August 1	108	101	99	80	81
August 18	98	97	86	76	77

Note: All figures are in degrees Fahrenheit.

This variation in temperatures holds the key to trout fishing in Arizona. Were it not for the cooler temperatures found at higher elevations, you'd find few viable trout streams here.

The Mogollon Rim also produces plenty of cool springs that serve as the headwaters of many trout streams. Travel to the upper end of Tonto Creek, or to Christopher Creek, to see what happens at their source. These two streams and many more begin as springs at the foot of the Mogollon Rim.

HOW TO USE THIS BOOK

Rationale for the Geographical Areas

We have organized Arizona streams, rivers, and lakes into seven chapters based on the geography and climate of the region. Here is the rationale for the division.

In chapter 3, in The Valley of the Sun, you'll find fly-fishing opportunities within minutes of the huge sprawling urban area of Phoenix. Here, anglers have an opportunity to fly-fish and see hatches throughout the winter.

Just 90 miles north of the Phoenix metropolitan area, in the Verde Valley, you can fish most of the year and fish over hatches in late winter. The elevations of these mountain streams range from 3500 to 6000 feet. Chapter 4 describes these rivers—all accessible from the Cottonwood-Sedona area.

Just east of the Verde Valley and 100 miles northeast of Phoenix, you'll find the streams and rivers described in chapter 5, the Payson-Young area. Elevations in this area range from 4000 to 7000 feet, and the streams can be fished most of the year (except those located highest up on the Mogollon Rim).

We've grouped those streams that are within the White Mountain Apache Reservation (also called Fort Apache Indian Reservation on many maps) in chapter 6. All streams in this chapter require a tribal permit. Here you'll find many streams at 6000 feet or higher, where winter comes with a vengeance. Many of the streams and the roads we use to get to them are inaccessible until mid-May.

In chapter 7, High Country, we've grouped streams and rivers that are 200 miles or more northeast of Phoenix. Here you'll find streams and rivers at elevations over 7000 feet, along with some of the classic Western hatches. High Country streams are often inaccessible until mid- to late May depending on the snowmelt.

We have devoted an entire chapter, chapter 8, to Arizona's finest fishing—Lee's Ferry and the Colorado River. Located in the far northern part of Arizona, and 4 hours from the Phoenix area, the Colorado River is definitely in a class of its own.

Anglers will find much of Arizona's best trout fishing in its lakes. Most of these are found at elevations above 6000 feet. We've devoted chapter 9 to the most highly recommended stillwaters in Arizona.

Rating the Trout Streams of Arizona

Here is how we define our rating system of 1 through 10:

1. Don't even send your worst enemy to this stream.
2. You might want to get your feet wet on this one.
3. Spend a half day on this stream.
4. This one has some good hatches and stocked trout.
5. This streams holds some very good hatches and some holdover trout.
6. Spend some time exploring this one—it sports some great hatches and native trout.
7. This trout water holds several great hatches and a lot of native trout.
8. What are you waiting for?
9. Fish this one right away!
10. Quit work immediately and fish this stream!

We've given a rating to each stream in this book—they're a rough gauge of the quality of fishing you can expect. Streams rated lower than a 5 demand little attention, whereas those from 6 to 10 hold some good hatches and streambred trout. I haven't included any of the streams I ranked 1 to 3, however; if they're that low on the list, I chose to leave them out altogether. What are the best streams in the state? Both the Colorado

River at Lee's Ferry and the Black River are rated a 9, Oak Creek near Sedona is an 8, and parts of the White and Colorado Rivers are a 7. When it comes to lakes, Sunrise Lake rated an 8. You'll find each stream's and lake's rating at the top of its description.

Positives and Negatives

We've also listed the pluses and minuses of each Arizona stream and lake. Is the area scenic? Is approaching the stream treacherous? Does it get a lot of angling pressure? How about the size of the trout, the size of the hatches, and the numbers of trout you'll find rising to these hatches? These and other facts are listed under "Positives" and "Negatives" at the head of each stream description. These lists should give you a quick glimpse of each stream to help you determine whether or not you want to fish it.

Access

If you've never fly-fished on Arizona's rivers, streams, and lakes then you're in for a huge surprise. Every fishing trip here begins with a crucial question: How do I get to the water? Even after you're on a stream, fly-fishing it will often confront you with impassable gorges, cliffs, and boulder chokes, both upstream and down. You'll find you must repeatedly climb over treacherous terrain just to reach another section of the stream to fish. On innumerable occasions I've come close to losing my footing and sliding down the side of a canyon. Many of Arizona's waters are not for the faint of heart and certainly not for the older fly-fisher.

You'll note that at the beginning of each stream description, we've rated its access as "Difficult," "Fair," or "Good." Proceed with extreme caution on many canyon-type trout streams—the ones we've rated as "Difficult." A "Fair " grade suggests some possible trouble spots. Streams we've rated as "Good" should be safely accessible for most anglers. Please be aware that these ratings are meant only as a general guide, and be sure to prepare yourself by purchasing adequate topographical maps and talking to knowledgeable fellow anglers.

Best Times of Year to Fly Fish

You will indeed find diversity in this land of cactus and pines. Some streams on the Mogollon Rim and in the White Mountains average more than 100 inches of snow annually. You can't reach streams like Big Bonito, Chevelon, and East and West Clear Creeks until late April or May. Hannagan Meadows at an altitude of more than 9000 feet in far eastern Arizona holds snow into May. Yet other trout waters here offer fishing only during the cold months. Rivers like the upper Verde near

Cottonwood, for instance, warm considerably in summer and harbor only warm-water species.

For this reason, we list the best or most practical season of the year to fish each stream in its description. Thus, for the upper Verde River you'll see "F, W, Sp." That means your best times to fish this river are in fall (F), winter (W), and spring (Sp). Big Bonito Creek, on the other hand, lists "Sp, S, F" because it's inaccessible in the winter months.

Also, at the end of each stream description you'll find a hatch chart; chapter 2 includes one chart for all the lakes of Arizona. These hatch charts will tell you approximately what days and times you can expect hatches on that particular water.

Maps

For each stream or lake we've listed the page number in DeLorme's *Arizona Atlas* on which it can be found. DeLorme's maps are generally accurate and easy to use, and the atlas includes other useful information about the state. If you can't find an atlas readily in a book or map store, you can order one from DeLorme Mapping Company by calling 1-800-734-0363. We've also listed the national forest or reservation maps that will be most helpful for that area.

Please be aware that most dirt roads are not marked, and what's more, that road numbers are often not consistent from one set of maps to another. Given these difficulties, we've made the maps in this book as accurate and clear as possible, but we do not intend that you use them as your sole source of navigation. Within the constraints of a book page it is impossible to draw the detail you'll find on an atlas or road map. We advise that you have with you a DeLorme atlas as well as a USGS topographical map or one of the national forest maps we've mentioned in the stream headings.

A FINAL WORD

Arizona offers fly-fishers beautiful waters—but remember that these precious resources are even more valuable in a state that depends on scant rainfall to survive. The last chapter of this guide offers a perspective on what we can do to help preserve these waters, and we encourage you to get involved. Leave each stream as you found it; return those beautiful trout you catch; and above all, enjoy your fly fishing journey along some of the world's most beautiful stretches of water—Arizona's trout streams and rivers.

2

A Close Look at the Hatches

After fishing many of the streams, rivers, and lakes of Arizona, I've learned much about their hatches. Equally valuable have been studies conducted by the Arizona Department of Environmental Quality (DEQ) and Arizona Game and Fish Department (AGF). Without the excellent research on insect populations conducted by Patti Spindler for the DEQ and J. Novy of the AGF, determining which hatches occurred on which streams would have been impossible. The following charts summarize Arizona hatches; after most charts I've included additional information that should be valuable to fly-fishers.

EMERGENCE DATES IN ARIZONA

I've never seen emergence dates as mixed up as they are in Arizona. Indeed, this state can be divided into at least four different zones based on temperature and the timing of aquatic hatches. You can fly-fish in zones 1 and 2 the entire year. Zone 1 (chapter 3)—the Phoenix area, known as the Valley of the Sun—is unlike anywhere else in the nation. Hatches here appear the entire year. On rivers in the Phoenix area, like the Salt and lower Verde, I've seen trico hatches on Christmas and New Year's Days. Little blue-winged olives appear here throughout the winter. You can expect to see some of the heaviest blue-winged olive hatches occurring in January and February.

The Cottonwood area holds the streams and rivers found in zone 2 (chapter 4). Here temperatures stay a bit cooler than in the Phoenix area—but you can often fish through much of the winter. On streams like the

Table 2. Hatches on Arizona Streams and Rivers

Common Name—Dun	Scientific name	Date*	Size	Time of Day	Common name—Spinner
Little black stonefly	Eucapnopsis brevicauda	February–April	16	Afternoon	
Little blue-winged olive dun	Baetis intercalaris	January*–December	20–22	Afternoon	Rusty spinner (Early evening)
Little blue-winged olive dun	Acentrella turbida	January*–December	22–24	Afternoon	Rusty spinner (Early evening)
Early blue or Little blue-winged olive dun	Baetis tricaudatus	March–December	16–20	Afternoon	Rusty spinner
Little golden stonefly	Skawala parallela	April 1	14	Afternoon	
Blue quill	Paraleptophlebia memorialis	March–July	18	Morning	Dark brown spinner
Quill gordon	Epeorus longimanus	March–May	16	Afternoon	
Pale morning dun	Ephemerella inermis	March–June	16	Morning, afternoon, and evening	Pale morning spinner

Common name	Scientific name	Date	Size	Time	Spinner
Trico dun	*Tricorythodes minutus*	February*–December	24	Morning	Trico spinner (Mid- to late morning)
Trico dun	*Tricorythodes fictus*	February–December	20	Morning	Trico spinner (Mid- to late morning)
Speckled-winged dun	*Callibaetis americanus*	April–November	16	Morning	Speckle-winged spinner
Little brown stonefly	*Amphinemura* spp.	April 1	16	Afternoon	
Grannon (caddisfly)	*Brachycentrus occidentalis*	May 1	16	Evening	
Western green drake	*Drunella grandis*	May–July	12	Morning	Dark olive spinner (Afternoon)
Dark brown dun	*Cinygmula par*	May 15	16	Noon	Dark brown spinner
Dark brown dun	*Rhithrogena robusta*	May 25	10–12	Morning	Dark brown spinner
Blue-winged olive dun	*Drunella spinifera*	June 1	16	Noon	Dark olive spinner
Blue-winged olive dun	*Drunella flavilinea*	June 15	14		Dark olive spinner
Little blue-winged olive dun	*Baetis bicaudatus*	June 1	20	Afternoon	Rusty spinner
Black quill	*Leptophlebia* spp.	June 1	16	Afternoon	
Little yellow stonefly	*Sweltsa coloradensis*	June 1	16	Evening	
Green caddisfly	*Rhyacophila vagrita*	June 15	12–14	Evening	

* The earliest dates apply to the Salt and Verde Rivers

Table 2. Hatches on Arizona Streams and Rivers (cont.)

COMMON NAME—DUN	SCIENTIFIC NAME	DATE*	SIZE	TIME OF DAY	COMMON NAME—SPINNER
Yellow caddisfly	Oecetis spp.	June 15	14–16	Evening	
Dark brown dun	Ameletus velox	June 15	14	Late morning	Dark brown spinner
Brown caddisfly	Oecetis spp.	June 15	14–16	Evening	
Golden stonefly	Hesperoperla pacifica	June 15	4	Evening	
Blue quill	Paraleptophlebia heteronea	June 15	18	Morning	Dark brown spinner
Black quill	Choroterpes spp.	June 20	14	Evening	Quill Gordon spinner
Black quill	Traverella spp.	June 25	14		
Cream dun	Leptohyphes spp.	July 1	22–24	Morning	Cream spinner
Little white mayfly	Caenis spp.	July 1	24–26	Evening	Little cream spinner
Gray drake	Siphlonurus occidentalis	July 1	10	Afternoon	Gray drake spinner
Dark blue dun	Thraulodes bicornuta	July 1	14–16	Evening	Dark gray spinner

* The earliest dates apply to the Salt and Verde Rivers.

Table 3. Hatches on Arizona Lakes

COMMON NAME—DUN	SCIENTIFIC NAME	DATE	SIZE	TIME OF DAY	COMMON NAME—SPINNER
Little blue-winged olive dun	*Baetis tricaudatus*	April–May	18–24	Afternoon	Rusty spinner
Speckle-winged dun	*Callibaetis coloradensis*	May–September	14–18	Late morning	Speckle-winged spinner
Damselfly	*Enallagma* spp.	June	10–14	Morning	
Dark brown dun	*Ameletus* spp.	June	10–14	Morning	Dark brown spinner

The rusty spinner appears in April.

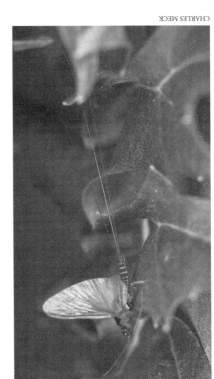

You'll find trico spinners on the Upper Verde River in February.

Upper Verde River at Cottonwood, you'll fly-fish over tricos, little blue-winged olives, and olive caddisflies in February.

The Payson area encompasses the third zone (chapter 5). You can fly-fish almost the entire year here, but expect to encounter snow and cold temperatures in January and February. I've found heavy little black stonefly and quill gordon hatches here in mid- and late March. Tricos don't emerge in zone 3 until June and July.

I include the Springerville-Alpine area in zone 4 (chapters 6 and 7). Here winter comes with a vengeance. Around the Greer area I've seen snowbanks remaining until mid-May. You'll see some hatches—like the blue quill—in April and May; trico hatches don't appear until mid-July. Here you'll also witness some of the famous western hatches, like the green drake, pale evening dun, and pale morning dun.

I construct emergence charts, like this one, for any area I fish, but I must caution you that charts give at best a rough estimate of the times you can expect to see various hatches. Fishing Arizona hatches requires even more caution. Remember when you read this chart that you're not looking at one zone and one series of emergence dates—you're looking at several regions and zones and the potential for tremendously varying emergence dates.

You'll find patterns for matching most of these hatches in chapter 10.

Table 4. Elevation and Density of Hatches in Arizona

SPECIES AND COMMON NAME	HIGH ELEV. STREAMS 6000'–10,000'	MED. ELEV. STREAMS 2000'–6000'	LOW ELEV. STREAMS Below 2000'
Baetis—Little blue-winged olive dun	H	H	H
Tricorythodes—Trico	M	H	H
Caenis—Little white mayfly	M	H	M
Paraleptophlebia—Blue quill	M	A	A
Drunella grandis— Western green drake	M	A	A
Ephemerella inermis—Pale morning dun	M	A	A
Siphlonurus occidentalis— Gray drake	L	L	A

SPECIES AND COMMON NAME	HIGH ELEV. STREAMS 6000'–10,000'	MED. ELEV. STREAMS 2000'–6000'	LOW ELEV. STREAMS Below 2000'
Heptagenia elegantula—Pale evening dun	M	M	A or L
Epeorus longimanus—Quill gordon	M	L to M	A
Cinygmula par—Dark brown dun	M	L to A	A
Choroterpes—Black quill	L or A	M to H	L or A
Ephemeralla spinifera—Blue-winged olive dun	L	A	A
Serratella micheneri—Blue-winged olive dun	A	M	L
Ameletus velox—Dark brown dun	M	A	A
Traverella spp.—Black quill	L	M	A
Thraulodes bicornuta—Dark blue dun	L	H	M
Amphinemura spp.—Little brown stonefly	M to H	L or A	A

A= Probably absent; L= Low population;
M= Medium population; H= High population

ELEVATION

As you can see, elevation affects Arizona hatches. In his master's thesis, "The Mayflies of Idaho," S.L. Jensen found that elevation affected the distribution of mayflies there; it appears to be an even more important factor in Arizona. Traveling from Phoenix northeast to the White Mountains takes you over not only 200 miles in distance, but also 7900 feet in elevation—from 1200 feet in the desert country to 9100 feet at Sunrise Lake. Some of the more widely known hatches of the West occur in Arizona only at the highest elevations. If you'd like to fish the western green drake or pale morning dun, for instance, then you've got to fly-fish on streams and rivers at 6000 feet or higher. In fact, I've never seen green drake hatches below 7000 feet. Many of the tributaries of the Little Colorado, Black, and Gila Rivers do hold these classic hatches, but you'll find them on few other streams, especially at lower elevations.

The blue quill (*Paraleptophlebia* spp.) also appears on high-altitude streams (with a couple of exceptions). I've seen great hatches of this mayfly in May on the Little Colorado River at the X-Diamond Ranch, at an elevation of about 7500 feet. If you want to fly-fish this hatch, then look for it on streams above 6000 feet. Workman Creek (elevation 6000 feet) near Young also holds a good blue quill hatch. The dark brown dun *(Ameletus velox)* also exhibits a preference for higher-altitude streams.

Look at the dark blue dun *(Thraulodes bicornuta)* for another example of an elevation-affected species. This hatch is usually heaviest on streams with elevations from 3000 to 6000 feet. High-elevation streams like Campbell Blue do hold hatches, but not many. Why haven't you heard about this mayfly before? Many of the mayflies found in the transitional zone between desert and high mountain—3000 to 6000 feet—are uncommon, or at least rarely mentioned, in fly-fishing literature.

Some stoneflies also seem to like higher-elevation streams. The little brown stonefly (*Amphimeura* spp.), for example, appears in heavier numbers in streams higher than 6000 feet.

Table 5. Mayfly Nymph Behavior

TYPE OF NYMPH	ABUNDANT	COMMON	PRESENT	ABSENT
Swimmers				
Baetis—Little blue-winged olive	X			
Callibaetis—Speckle-winged dun			X	
Isonychia—Slate drake				X
Siphlonurus—Gray drake			X	
Ameletus—Dark brown dun		X		
Crawlers				
Seratella micheneri—Blue-winged olive			X	
Ephemerella inermis—Pale morning dun			X	

Type of Nymph	Abundant	Common	Present	Absent
Drunella grandis—Western green drake			X	
Tricorythodes—Trico		X		
*Leptohyphes**		X		
Leptophlebia—Black quill	X			
Paraleptophlebia—Blue quill		X		
Caenis—Little white mayfly		X		
Traverella—Black quill			X	
Choroterpes—Black quill	X			
Clingers				
Cinygmula—Dark brown dun		X		
Epeorus—Quill gordon		X		
Heptagenia—Pale evening dun	X			
Stenonema—Light cahill				X
Stenacron—Light cahill				X
Burrowers				
Hexagenia—Hex				X
Ephoron—White mayfly				X
Ephemera—Drake				X

*No common name

MAYFLY NYMPHS

In table 5 you see mayfly genera listed according to the behavior of their nymphs. If the nymph clings to a rock, it's called a *clinger*. If it burrows in the gravel, then it's a *burrower*. *Swimmers* swim freely; *crawlers* crawl around on the bottom. The most common type of mayfly in Arizona is the crawler.

Arizona streams have few burrowing mayflies. In fact, I didn't note any of the mayflies that generally burrow into the substrate in either the research or my observations. Why? Look at the substrate, or lack of it, on many Arizona streams—not the perfect environment for burrowers.

There's no need for you to look for hatches like the brown drake (*Ephemera* spp.), hex (*Hexagenia* spp.), or white mayfly (*Ephoron* spp.). These mayflies don't appear in any numbers in Arizona.

Table 6. Percent of Mayflies, Stoneflies, Caddisflies, and Midges Found on Streams

STREAM	MAYFLIES	CADDISFLIES	STONEFLIES	MIDGES
Black River—East Fork	17	38	1	37
Black River—West Fork	43	7	3	29
Blue River	31	10	8	14
Canyon Creek	60	4	0	16
Cherry Creek	32	16	0	44
Chevelon (Long Tom) Creek	38	2	4	48
East Clear Creek— Kinder Crossing	56	13	0	17
East Verde River	41	1	0	56
Haigler Creek	26	33	0	14
Little Colorado River— East Fork	6	9	7	66
Little Colorado River— Mainstream	43	15	11	15
Little Colorado River— South Fork	28	3	7	52
Little Colorado River— West Fork	18	2	3	74
Oak Creek	45	6	0	7
Oak Creek—West Fork	31	8	0	42
Reynolds Creek	15	7	3	72
San Francisco River	71	4	0	22
Tonto Creek	28	6	4	61
Verde River—Upper	59	25	0	3

STREAM	MAYFLIES	CADDISFLIES	STONEFLIES	MIDGES
Webber Creek	33	2	0	62
West Clear Creek	48	12	5	18
Wet Beaver Creek	46	4	0	17
Workman Creek	19	6	41	13

Note: Numbers in the rows don't add up to 100 percent because other aquatic insects, such as beetles, have not been included.

Adapted from "Using Ecoregions for Explaining Macroinvertebrate Community Distribution Among Reference Sites in Arizona, 1992," a survey conducted by the Water Quality Division of the Arizona Department of Environmental Quality.

STONEFLIES AND CADDISFLIES

Stoneflies do not make up an important part of a trout's diet in many southwestern streams. Only two of the streams (Workman Creek and the Little Colorado River) listed in table 6 show double-digit percentages of this downwing. Among some of the more common stoneflies are the little yellow

The little blue-winged olive is found on the Salt River all winter and is common throughout Arizona.

CHARLES MECK

stone *(Skwala parallela),* the little black stone *(Encapnopsis brevicauda),* and the little brown stone *(Amphinemura* spp.). You'll see the little black stone-flies on a number of streams and rivers—like Oak, Tonto, and Christopher Creeks—in March and early April. Unlike many other stoneflies, which emerge on or near the shore, little black stoneflies often appear in the middle of the stream. Trout do often feed on them—that is, if you don't encounter high muddy waters in early spring. The little brown stonefly also appears in numbers on some streams, and make certain you carry some size 16 Little Yellow Stoneflies to copy the *Skwala parallela* hatch on Arizona streams. These pale downwings often appear in June and July.

Caddisflies are well represented in state streams; the DEQ study on which table 6 is based found 49 different caddisfly species on Arizona streams. Carrying Grannoms *(Brachycentrus* spp.), Spotted Sedges (*Hydropsyche* spp.), Dark Tan Caddis (*Polycentropus* spp.), and Green Caddis *(Rhyacophila* spp.) will allow you to copy many of these hatches. The Salt and Verde Rivers hold great caddisfly hatches that appear as early as February; I've seen the Salt come alive on March evenings with early hatches of grannoms. These caddis usually have black or green bodies, so carry plenty of black- and green-bodied downwings in sizes 14 and 16. Expect to see good caddisfly hatches on Eagle and Haigler Creeks and the upper Verde River.

MIDGES

In this book you'll find little mention of midges or *Chironomids*—but this does not mean these diminutive insects aren't important on Arizona streams and lakes. There are 111 different midge species in Arizona. You'll find them on various waters throughout the year—many of them the Southwest's best trout streams. During winter look for these hatches on streams at the most comfortable time of day—midafternoon. In winter the most common body color seems to be dark gray. In the hot summer months these hatches appear on lakes and streams at dusk or dawn. You'll find cream, green, and yellow body colors common throughout summer.

Expect to see plenty of *Chironomid* on Cherry, Chevelon, Reynolds, and Webber Creeks, and on the Colorado, Little Colorado, and East Verde Rivers.

In chapter 10 I've listed some patterns for *Chironomid*. Don't overlook the Griffith's Gnat—it works well during midge activity.

Table 7. Major Aquatic Insects on Selected Streams, River, and Lakes

BODY OF WATER	MAJOR HATCH OR MAJOR AQUATIC INSECT	TYPE*
Black River, East Fork	*Brachycentrus*—Grannom	C
Black River, West Fork	*Baetis*—Little blue-winged olive dun	M
Blue River	*Microcylloepus*—Aquatic beetle	B
Campbell Blue Creek	*Baetis*—Little blue-winged olive dun	M
Canyon Creek	*Baetis*—Little blue-winged olive dun	M
Cherry Creek	*Baetis*—Little blue-winged olive dun	M
Chevelon Creek	*Leptophlebia*—Black quill	M
Eagle Creek	*Hydropsyche*—Tan caddisfly	C
East Clear Creek	*Baetis*—Little blue-winged olive dun	M
East Verde River	*Baetis*—Little blue-winged olive dun	M
Haigler Creek	*Ceratopogoginae*—Biting Midge	D
Little Colorado River	*Baetis*—Little blue-winged olive dun	M
Little Colorado River, West Fork	*Similiidae*—Black fly	D
Little Colorado River, East Fork	*Eukieferiella*—Midge	MI
Lower Salt River	*Baetis*—Little blue-winged olive dun	M
Oak Creek	*Tricorythodes*—Trico	M
Oak Creek, West Fork	*Caenis*—Little white mayfly	M
Reynolds Creek	*Similiidae*—Black fly	D
San Francisco River	*Traverella*— Black quill	M
Tonto Creek	*Similiidae*—Black fly	D
Upper Verde River	*Baetis*—Little blue-winged olive dun	M
Webber Creek	*Similiidae*—Black fly	D
Workman Creek	*Amphinemura*—Little brown	S
West Clear Creek	*Baetis*—Little blue-winged olive dun	M
Wet Beaver Creek	*Baetis*—Little blue-winged olive dun	M

*Key: M = Mayfly; C = Caddisfly ; S= Stonefly ; B= Beetle ; MI = Midge; D = other Diptera

Early blue photographed on Oak Creek

ARIZONA'S MOST COMMON HATCHES

Several years ago Arizona Game and Fish conducted studies on some of the trout streams in the White Mountains including the Little Colorado and Black Rivers. The most abundant mayflies they found were the little blue-winged olive (*Baetis* spp.), blue quill or mahogany dun (*Paraleptophlebia* spp.), dark brown dun (*Ameletus* spp.), pale evening dun *(Heptagenia elegantula)*, and trico *(Tricorythodes minutus)*. They even found green drakes *(Drunella grandis)* and pale morning duns *(Ephemerella inermis)* on some of these high elevation waters.

By far the most common hatch on Arizona streams and rivers is the little blue-winged olive dun (*Baetis* spp.). On rivers like the Salt the common hatch is the *B. intercalis*, which appears just about all winter long. The mating adult (rusty spinner) can be more important in January and February. You'll find a second species, *B. tricaudatus*, on many streams in the Sedona-Payson area from March through April. Local fly-fishers call this hatch the "early blue." *Baetis* mayflies can be found in good numbers on streams of all elevations. Hannagan Creek, for instance—at an elevation of 9000 feet— holds one of the heaviest little blue-winged olive dun hatches in the state.

Probably the second most common hatch is the trico *(Tricorythodes minutus* and *T. fictus)*. Indeed, I'm continually amazed at the wide distribution of tricos in Arizona; these small mayflies can be found on just about every stream in the state. Desert rivers like the Salt and lower Verde hold excellent trico hatches; because of their low elevations and relatively warm temperatures, hatches of these two mayflies appear throughout much of winter. On the upper Verde in Cottonwood I've seen tricos in both size 20 and size 24. These large and small tricos are members of the same species—*(T. fictus)*—and they appear in the air and fall at the same time. On higher-elevation streams like Haigler and Tonto Creeks the trico appears in June. Still, you'll find trico hatches heaviest on trout waters with elevations lower than 6000 feet.

Many Arizona trout waters other than the Verde River hold great trico hatches. Rivers like the Little Colorado, Black, and Salt, along with most of their tributaries, boast good trico numbers. And tricos can appear in Arizona any time of the year. Hatches on the Salt sometimes occur in December and January; on the Verde near Cottonwood tricos first appear for the year in late February. Tricos are temperature-driven, so if you hit a cool winter, the upper Verde River's hatches might not appear until early March. Trico hatches on the Little Colorado and Black Rivers begin around early July.

The blue quill probably ranks as the third most common mayfly hatch on Arizona's trout streams. Just about every stream and river I've fly-fished in late April and May hold a good hatch. Look for this hatch to appear in late morning.

PLANNING YOUR FISHING TRIP TO MEET THE HATCHES

All of the tables here should help you plan your own trips and tell you what hatches you'll see. For example, travel to some of the forks of the Little Colorado or Black Rivers in early to late June and you'll likely see some pale morning duns and green drakes in the morning (tables 2 and 4). If you'd like to see emerging stoneflies, try fishing Workman Creek in April (table 7). Table 7 shows that the heaviest hatch on this small stream is the little brown stonefly, and table 2 indicates that the hatch appears in April.

If you're looking for a hatch of pale evening duns (*Heptagenia* spp.), fish streams and rivers above 2000 feet. Some of the heavier hatches of this mayfly appear on streams with elevations from 5000 to 8000 feet.

Many Arizona waters hold heavy little white mayfly (*Caenis* spp.) hatches. You'll find this diminutive insect (sizes 22 to 26) heaviest on

streams with elevations from 3000 to 6000 feet. These almost impercep-
tible mayflies often appear at dusk on midsummer evenings.

When you know what hatches to expect, you can carry several patterns to match them—Little Blue-Winged Olive Duns (sizes 20 to 24);
Tricos (sizes 20 to 24); Pale Evening Duns (sizes 16 and 18).

Also bring plenty of downwings with you to imitate stoneflies and
caddisflies. Try Black Caddis (size 14 and 16); Green Caddis (sizes 12 to
16); Tan Caddis (sizes 12 to 16); Olive Caddis (size 12 and 14); and Little
Yellow stoneflies (size 16).

3

Trout Fishing in the Valley of the Sun

Every day that I'm caught inside by winter weather I dream of fly-fishing. Guess what? Luckily, I've found one place in the United States where I can fish every winter day—most of the time with temperatures hovering around 65 degrees and water temperatures in the mid- to upper 50s. And to top it off, most days will have plenty of sunshine.

Yes, the Valley of the Sun has a lot going for it, but despite its potential to have a fantastic fishery, it looks like this area will fumble the ball. Let me explain. The Salt River has the potential to be one of the top tailwaters in the nation, and its weather would draw thousands of fly-fishers to the area—but getting the diverse groups that control this river to agree on its potential is another story. I've already described the conflicts, for instance, between the Game and Fish Department and the Salt River Project (SRP) (see "The Downside" in chapter 1). Another example is the state's plan to create a catch-and-release area from the Stewart Mountain Dam downriver to the Water User's Recreation Area. But as I write, this planned catch-and-release area seems to be in jeopardy. Recreational tubers usually enter the Salt River at the Water User's Area. If plans progress, guess where they'll enter? You got it, at the base of the dam—just where the specially regulated water is to be sited.

The future indeed looks grim for the Salt River. Only if Arizona Game and Fish agrees to reimburse the SRP for a guaranteed minimum flow throughout the year will this potentially great tailwater survive. Only through the pressure of interested anglers and sportsmen's groups will a unrealized tailwater become a reality.

To add to the Salt's problems, the Fort McDowell Indian tribe recently

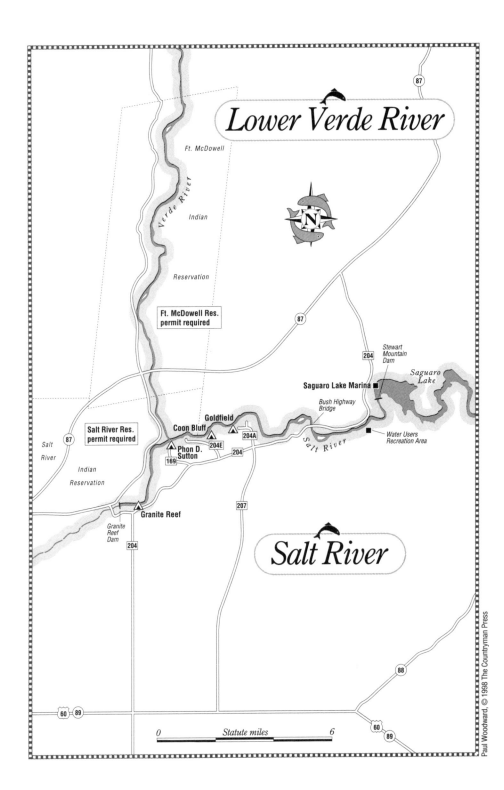

Lower Verde River

Ft. McDowell

Verde River

Indian

Reservation

Ft. McDowell Res.
permit required

87

87

204 Stewart
Mountain
Dam

Saguaro
Lake

Saguaro Lake Marina ■

Bush Highway
Bridge

Salt River Res.
permit required

Salt
River

Indian

Reservation

Goldfield

Coon Bluff

204E

204A

204

Salt River

■ Water Users
Recreation Area

Phon D.
Sutton

169

207

Granite Reef

Granite
Reef
Dam

204

Salt River

88

60 89

60

89

0   Statute miles   6

closed the lower Verde River, which flows just 20 miles east of Phoenix. The reason? Environmental concerns. These concerns are certainly valid, but you and I know that it's not fly-fishers who've trashed the banks along the Verde River.

Nevertheless you will find some good fishing on the Salt and lower Verde Rivers.

LOWER VERDE RIVER

Rating: 5
Access: Good
Seasons: F, W, S
Maps: DeLorme p. 58, Tonto National Forest maps
Regulations: Tribal permit required
Positives: Great fishing weather all winter long, easy access to Phoenix area
Negatives: Flow varies tremendously, a warm-water fishery in late spring and summer, not stocked consistently, few hiding spots for trout

My son, Bryan, and I have spent the past few Christmas mornings fly-fishing the Verde River at the Fort McDowell Indian Reservation just outside Phoenix. We arrive by 8 AM, purchase our tribal permit, and head down to the river. Rarely do we see another angler on these holiday fishing trips. Yet each Christmas we've fly-fished under bright blue skies with air temperatures near 60 degrees by 10 AM. And each Christmas we've spotted a few tricos in mating swarms just above some fast-water stretches. This past year two bald eagles sat on a nearby tree to watch us fish. And every year we catch close to a dozen trout each. Not a bad way to spend Christmas morning.

The lower Verde is indeed a put-and-take trout river. Because the bottom has little structure, trout seem to migrate shortly after they're stocked. It's really the kind of stream you'd expect to flow through a desert—a sand bottom with few permanent pools. In fact, I know of only two pools on the entire lower Verde that contain a bottom where trout hide. One is about ½ mile below the AZ 87 bridge, the other ½ mile above the bridge. Still, you can experience some great fly-fishing on the lower Verde.

You'll find hatches here, too. In addition to some tricos, you'll find a steady daily parade of little blue-winged olives emerging. In the late afternoon I've seen trout rise to the spent mating adult of this species, the rusty spinner. I've also seen trout rise on occasion to a small black caddis in

The Verde River near Phoenix

January. If you enjoy dry fly-fishing and you hit the river at exactly the right time, you might even see trout rising to a small midge just before midday. On several trips I've taken a dozen or more trout on a size 24 Dark Gray Midge pattern.

Gordon Brick and Fred Brauburger (both of the Phoenix area), along with Virgil Bradford (of Santa Fe, New Mexico), fish the lower Verde many times throughout the winter. We've experienced some days where we've caught and released 50 to 60 rainbow trout.

There's about 4 or 5 miles of stock water on the lower Verde. Both the Verde and the Salt suffer when the volume of flow is too high or low. The river warms considerably in April and becomes a warm-water fishery until November.

But recently, the lower Verde has fallen on hard times. Normally the stream is stocked twice a month. In 1997–98 it received only one planting a month from November through March—and I question that one planting. On several occasions I've fished all morning without a strike. It seems when authorities stock this part of the Verde, they often dump the entire contents of the stocking truck at one location—and often nobody knows where this is. Until the trout are distributed more evenly, the lower Verde will continue to be relatively unproductive.

The best fishing on the Verde is from a mile above the AZ 87 bridge to a mile below. To access these areas take Fort McDowell Road north off AZ 87. After 200 feet, turn right onto An-Sha Lane to reach the bridge and lower portion; travel 1.1 miles to Sandtrap Road to get to the middle section; 1.7 miles up Fort McDowell Road you'll find a parking area next to the river. A fourth section, 2.3 miles up the highway, is off Harquahala Road. Fish the section just downriver from the Public Works Building. You do need to purchase a tribal permit to fish the lower Verde on the Fort McDowell Reservation. You can get it at the Baja gas station on the reservation. Lenor Duran, assistant manager, will tell you where to fish and when and where authorities have planted trout.

Don't fish the lower Verde if it's the least bit off color. I've found extremely poor fly-fishing every time the water had just a suggestion of turbidity. Also check on the water flow. If it's higher than 300 cubic feet per second, don't even think of fly-fishing. You can check the level of the lower Verde and the Salt by calling (602) 236-5929.

You'll often find a lot of trout where the Verde enters the Salt, at Phon D. Sutton. You can access this area from the Bush Highway (204). If you fish the final mile of the river before it enters the Salt River, you must buy a permit from the Salt River Reservation.

Important Note: **As this book was going to press, the Lower Verde was closed to fly-fishing by tribal authorities.** There is reason to believe that this will not be a permanent situation, but make sure you check with the reservation to find out if it has reopened before you go.

BEST TIMES TO FISH THE HATCHES

January 1–April 30
Dark Gray Caddis: afternoon, size 20
Tan Caddis: afternoon, size 14
Little Blue-Winged Olive Dun: afternoon, size 20
Rusty Spinner: evening, size 20
Trico: morning, size 24
Green Caddis: morning, size 18
Pale Morning Dun: morning and evening, size 18

May 1–June 30
Trico: morning, size 24
Pale Morning Dun: morning and evening, sizes 16 and 18

October 1–January 1
Little Blue-Winged Olive Dun: afternoon, size 20
Trico: morning, size 24

SALT RIVER

Rating: 6
Access: Good
Seasons: Year-round
Maps: DeLorme p. 58, Tonto National Forest maps
Positives: Some holdover trout, tailwater fishery below Stewart
Mountain Dam, well stocked, a good little blue-winged olive dun
hatch, fantastic weather all winter, easily accessible
Negatives: Becomes a warm water fishery in summer a few miles
downriver from the dam, Salt River Project often limits water
flow to 8 cubic feet per second in winter, severely limiting trout
fishing; crowded on weekends, lots of tubers in warmer months,
water flow varies considerably

Can you imagine how it feels fly-fishing with air temperatures near 100 degrees? Try fly-fishing the Salt River just 25 miles east of Phoenix on any given day in June or July and you'll quickly find out. And if you're wondering how a stream in the sweltering Valley of the Sun can hold trout, the answer is Stewart Mountain Dam. Authorities added a bottom release to it and the water flowing out comes from the bottom of 125-foot-deep Saguaro Lake. Because of that bottom release this tailwater holds trout even in summer. Fish a mile or so below the dam, even in October, and you'll catch some trout planted the previous spring. Yes, the Salt does boast some holdovers.

In a recent article in *Fly Fisherman* magazine, I described how the trout-stocking program began on the Salt River. The Arizona Game and Fish Department has stocked the Salt in summer since 1974. Winter plantings of trout didn't begin until 1991, when Tom McMahon and Jim Warnecke, both with the Game and Fish Department, came up with an idea: Why not stock trout in the tailwater below Saguaro Lake for winter fishing? The area had two things going for it, said Tom McMahon: "We've got water and it's next to a huge sprawling urban area." Phoenix, Mesa, Scottsdale, and Tempe are less than an hour away. So the department surveyed anglers using the river; most favored a cold-water fishery.

Winter plantings began. But Arizona trout fishing has many problems. Just about every drop of water flowing in the Verde and Salt Rivers ends up in one of the canals that line the Phoenix landscape. Because water is so precious in this desert, the two rivers serving the area suffer. On many winter days I've seen only a trickle of water flow in the Salt River below Saguaro Lake.

RON DUNGAN

Indian petroglyph in Salt River Canyon

Indeed, civilization has been extremely unkind to this once proud river. Walk the riverbed just below Granite Reef Dam and you'll probably find only rocks—the river's path nothing more than a dry bed. After periods of high runoff and heavy rains are usually the only times that you'll see any flow beyond that point. During November and December you'll often find the river flowing below Saguaro Lake at a measly 8 cubic feet per second (cfs). Recently the Salt River Project (SRP) has also severely limited flow in January, February, and March. In the past the SRP allowed 300 to 400 cfs to flow out of the lake, so you can see that a trivial 8 cfs causes problems with this river as a trout fishery. If the Salt had a more constant flow, it would greatly improve. Anglers who have fly-fished it since it received its first planting of trout talk about a great season of trout fishing they experienced a few years ago; because of a constant release from the Stewart Mountain Dam, they'll tell you, many anglers caught holdover trout in the 15- to 16-inch category. Several years ago Berkley Power Bait stocked the river with about 200 rainbows over 15 inches long; many measured 18 to 20 inches long. For two weeks Gordon Brick, Fred Brauburger, and I caught some of these lunkers. Then authorities lowered the flow to 8 cfs and the fly-fishing was gone.

What happens when there's a constant flow in the Salt all year long? About four years ago Arizona received more than its normal amount of

The Salt River near Phoenix

precipitation. The lower Salt River had continuous flows for more than 18 months. Fisheries Chief Joe Janisch and Public Information Officer Rory Aikens said that some of the employees in Game and Fish caught 2- and 3-pound trout that year—even when the daytime temperatures soared above the century mark.

I believe the Salt River could rise to the national prominence if it had a good flow all year. First, the coldest temperature I've ever recorded on the Salt was 52 degrees. With minimum temperatures like that trout grow rapidly throughout the year. Also, it's very fertile and holds several prolific hatches in midwinter. Even in December, January, and February you'll see tricos on this water. One New Year's Day I fished the lower section of the river, just above Granite Reef; that morning I saw a few hundred tricos in a mating cluster. And at this same time of year the Salt also boasts a hatch of little blue-winged olives each day. Near dusk in January and February you'll find the spinner of the little blue-winged olive, the rusty spinner, falling to the surface. Arrive at the Water User's Recreation Area around 5:30 PM in January and February and you'll find trout rising to spent spinners. Can you imagine how heavy the trico and little blue-winged olive duns hatches would be if a more constant flow occurred year-round?

Can anything be done about the inconsistent flow on the Salt River? Gary Yamaguchi thinks so. Gary has organized a group of interested anglers in the Phoenix area to work with Arizona Game and Fish and the Salt River Project to create a more constant flow throughout the year. Support his effort by contacting G. Yamaguchi Flyfishing, PO Box 51375, Phoenix, AZ 85076. If you're even thinking of fishing the Salt River, you've got to become involved.

You can access the Salt easily from the Bush Highway (204). I prefer fly-fishing the river at the Water User's Recreation Area, about a mile below Stewart Dam. You'll find a lot of anglers in this area, but it also holds a good number of hatches, trout, and deep pools and riffles—that is, when authorities allow enough water out of the dam. In this area the Salt reminds me of dozens of other western trout rivers.

A mile downriver you can readily reach the Salt from the Bush Highway bridge. Locals call this area Blue Point. Game and Fish usually plants trout in this area. Here I prefer fly-fishing a few hundred yards above the bridge. Other access spots (and camping areas) downriver include the Phon D. Sutton, Coon Bluff, and Goldfield. Coon Bluff is almost a mile upriver from the Phon D. Sutton. In another mile beyond that you'll find the access road (204A) to Goldfield. Fish the rapids just a couple of hundred yards below the parking lots at Goldfield and Coon Bluff. Here you'll find some deep, fast water and some great hatches. Look for the little blue-winged olive in the afternoon and its adult, the rusty spinner, to fill the air just above the rapids just at dusk from December through February. At the Coon Bluff area I caught several trout in the 5- to 8-inch class that almost looked like they were holdovers or streambred.

At Phon D. Sutton you'll find some fishing pressure but, again, plenty of planted trout. At this access spot, the Verde River enters the Salt. From this point downstream the Salt takes on the appearance of the Verde—a typical desert stream. If I fly-fish in the Phon D. Sutton area I usually hike downriver a mile, where there are some productive riffles. At the Phon D. Sutton near dusk you can experience some good match-the-hatch opportunities for downwings in March and April. And just ask Tom Heatherington of Pittsburgh, Pennsylvania, about the caddis hatch in late March. Tom was fly-fishing the stream one March when, late in the evening, caddisflies returned to the surface to lay their eggs. In less than an hour he landed four trout on a dry fly. As he landed the last fish, just at dusk, the Hale-Bopp comet appeared over his shoulder. What a fitting way to end an excellent hour of fishing to rising trout!

Don't overlook the Granite Reef Dam section of the river. (All together, there's about 10 miles of fishing from the Granite Reef Dam upriver to the Stewart Mountain Dam.) You'll find plenty of tubers floating near Granite Reef Dam during summer, so plan to fish just before sunrise. If the flow isn't too high you can wade across the upper end of this small impoundment and fish a fairly deep channel. If all else fails I usually end up at this section of the river. Fish the upper end of the dam where there's still some movement to the water. Jay Whitmore of nearby Mesa fishes this section frequently and catches a lot of trout. With a flow of 300 cfs or more the Salt River ranges from 40 to 60 feet wide in its upper end, and 50 to 80 feet wide below Phon D. Sutton. With the flow reduced to 8 cfs the Salt averages 20 to 30 feet wide.

You'll see lots of fish rising on an average day on the Salt River—but watch closely and you'll find that nearly 99 percent of them are desert suckers and roundtail chubs. Look for trout rising at dusk, especially when the rusty spinners fall in January and February.

What does the future hold for this tailwater in the Valley of the Sun? If the SRP and Arizona Game and Fish can reach an agreement, the future looks bright. For the next several years Game and Fish will check the effects of a continuous flow in winter, which should benefit the aquatic insect population. In a few years the river could hold tremendous trico and little blue-winged olive dun hatches throughout the year. In a few years you could find holdover trout in the upper few miles of the river; finding streambred rainbows is not out of the question. And Game and Fish could make a catch-and-release fly-fishing-only area in the first mile of the river below the dam. Wouldn't it be a great idea to make the *next* couple of miles an all-tackle catch-and-release section? Authorities could study both sections to determine the effects of both tackle and releasing trout.

If plans progress the Salt River has the potential to become one of the Southwest's top tailwaters.

BEST TIME TO FISH THE HATCHES

November 1–December 31
Trico: morning, size 24 (spotty)
Little Blue-Winged Olive Dun: morning and afternoon, sizes 20 and 22

January 1–April 30
Trico: morning and afternoon, size 24 (spotty)
Little Blue-Winged Olive Dun: morning and afternoon, sizes 20 and 22
Blue Quill: morning and afternoon, size 18
Pale Evening Dun: evening, sizes 16 and 18
Green Caddis: evening, size 14
Black Caddis: evening, size 16

Little Rusty Dun (afternoon) and Rusty Spinner (evening), sizes 22 and 24

May 1–June 30
Trico: morning, size 24 (spotty)
Blue Quill: morning, size 18
Little Blue-Winged Olive Dun: afternoon, size 20
Little Green Caddis: evening, size 16

July 1–August 31
Trico: morning, size 24 (spotty)

September 1–October 30
Trico: morning, size 24 (spotty)
Little Blue-Winged Olive Dun: morning and afternoon, sizes 20 and 22

4

North-Central Arizona—
The Verde Valley

Awesome red rock scenery—that's what you'll see in the Sedona-Cottonwood area, and to top it off, you've got fly-fishing all year. Hit the upper Verde River in early March and you'll see tricos falling and trout rising. You'll also find trout rising on Oak Creek, the West Fork of Oak, and Wet Beaver Creek to little black stoneflies and quill gordons in late winter and early spring. On late-March days these aquatic insects emerge much of the afternoon. Most of the streams I'll discuss here can be fished all winter—another advantage. Throughout much of the season you'll see little blue-winged olive duns appearing in the afternoon. Don't fish any stream in the state, especially Oak Creek, without a good supply of size 20 and 22 Little Blue-Winged Olive patterns.

The Verde Valley trout waters have all this going for them and they're only 90 miles north of Phoenix. And guess what? The area also has something for the entire family, even those who don't fish. You'll find the Lazy Horse, Jerome, Slide Rock, Red Rock, and Fort Verde State Parks interesting and educational. Pete Sesow, executive director of the Cottonwood Chamber of Commerce, knows the area's attractions well, and he'll tell you that just about every town here maintains a museum. The town of Cottonwood includes a historic area called Old Town. And if you haven't visited Sedona then you've really missed something. The splendor of this area's red rocks draws thousands of tourists annually.

If area streams receive adequate snowfall during the winter months, be prepared for major runoff in March or early April. I've seen days—no, weeks—when *all* these Verde Valley streams and rivers ran high and muddy. Contact the Cottonwood or Sedona Chamber of Commerce for more information on water conditions.

UPPER VERDE RIVER

Rating: 6
Access: Good
Seasons: F, W, Sp
Maps: DeLorme p. 41, Coconino National Forest maps
Regulations: Parking permit required for Dead Horse Ranch State Park
Positives: Great trico hatch from late February through April, well stocked with trout, easy access
Negatives: Warms up in summer, put-and-take river, heavily fished after every stocking, gets muddy from runoff in March

Craig Josephson had just landed at Sky Harbor Airport in Phoenix. He had a few days to spend with me in the land of the sun before he had to return to snowy Syracuse, New York. I planned to take him 90 miles north of Phoenix to fly-fish the upper Verde River near Cottonwood, Arizona. Weather forecasters predicted a great day for Phoenix—temperatures on that mid-February Saturday were to rise into the mid-70s. Even Cottonwood was expected to peak out near 70 degrees. It took us just two hours to travel up I-17 to Dead Horse Ranch State Park (exit 1-17 on AZ 260). When we arrived at the river we were amazed at the number of anglers out on this Saturday morning. The upper Verde does indeed get plenty of angling pressure—especially on weekends.

Shortly after we arrived at the water we saw small mayflies emerge. At first I thought they were little blue-winged olives. But by 10 AM hundreds of these insects were emerging in the pool in front of Craig and me, so I quickly grabbed one and blurted out to Craig, in amazement, "these are trico duns!" Trico duns in mid-February? A winter trico hatch? I had seen a few tricos appear on the Salt near Phoenix in December and January, but never in numbers large enough to bring trout to the surface. By 10:30, however, trico spinners began to fall onto the surface and a half-dozen trout rose to this early-season feast right in front of me. Craig and I hurriedly tied on Trico Spinners and began casting. I missed the first trout that rose to my pattern—but hooked the second. I wanted so desperately to land that fish. When I did it was a first for me—

Fishing on the Verde River in spring

a trout caught on a Trico pattern in midwinter.

We headed upriver to the next pool and found two pods of 20 to 30 trout in each, rising to spent spinners. Trico spinners continued to fall onto the surface for two more hours that morning. Craig and I continued to match this hatch and landed more than a dozen trout. What a midwinter day of fly-fishing! That's one that will go down in my memory, and Craig's, too.

Was that intense trico hatch in February an aberration? I returned to the upper Verde two weeks later, in early March, and I didn't have to wait long to get my answer. By 10 AM a heavy swarm of trico spinners formed a sphere 10 feet above a riffle in front of me. The trout seemed to know that the spinner fall would soon appear, and they began feeding almost as soon as the first trico hit the surface. The spinner fall again lasted for more than two hours, with dozens of trout breaking the surface to feed on these tiny egg layers.

Arizona Game and Fish stocks the upper Verde every other week from November through March. I'm undecided as to what happens to these trout after they're stocked. I've seen pools near Dead Horse Ranch State Park that held 50 to 100 trout shortly after stocking—but when I returned to the spot a week later I neither caught nor saw a trout.

By April or May water temperatures in the upper and lower Verde River rise into the 70s, and the river becomes a warm-water fishery. Trout leave the main stem for one of the cold tributaries.

You'll find good access at Dead Horse Ranch State Park (which charges a fee for parking). You can also access the upper Verde at Tuzigoot National Monument, a couple of miles upriver from Cottonwood. I've seen tricos here in late February, and you'll find parking and good fishing. Here look for a long, slow pool; fish this pool from its western or southern side on a March evening and you'll find plenty of trout rising to midges and caddisflies.

Another access point is between Cottonwood and Camp Verde at Thousand Trails. Turn at Thousand Trails onto a poor dirt road before you get to the Thousand Trails Resort. Two other locations in the Camp Verde area are the White Bridge (AZ 260) and Beasley Flats (off Salt Mine Road). The latter has a developed picnic area.

If you fish the upper Verde for any length of time you'll probably catch plenty of Verde trout—a type of chub found in the river that likes to take a fly. These chubs readily feed on trico spinners. The river gets warm in the summer and doesn't hold a resident population of trout; it depends totally on its stockings, which usually begin in the Wet Beaver Creek tributary in April and continue until July. The stream warms considerably in summer, so often stocking isn't resumed until October and November.

Oak Creek enters the Verde between Cottonwood and Camp Verde. Beaver Creek enters at Camp Verde, and West Clear Creek a few miles downriver. East Verde River, also stocked with trout, flows into the Verde 10 miles below West Clear Creek. All of these, along with one of Beaver Creek's tributaries, the Wet Beaver, hold trout.

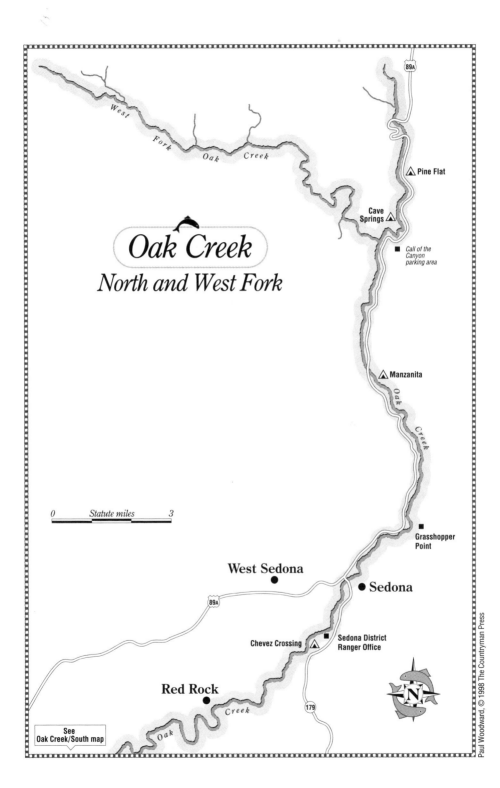

Oak Creek
North and West Fork

West Fork Oak Creek

89A

△ Pine Flat

Cave Springs △

■ *Call of the Canyon parking area*

△ Manzanita

Oak Creek

0   *Statute miles*   3

■ Grasshopper Point

West Sedona
●

● **Sedona**

89A

Chevez Crossing △   ■ Sedona District Ranger Office

Red Rock
●   *Creek*

Oak

179

N

See
Oak Creek/South map

Paul Woodward, © 1998 The Countryman Press

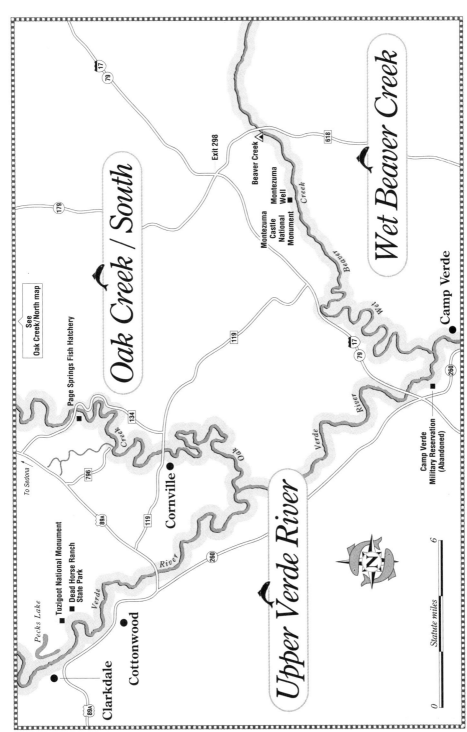

Oak Creek / South

Wet Beaver Creek

Upper Verde River

See
Oak Creek/North map

Page Springs Fish Hatchery

To Sedona

Peeks Lake

Tuzigoot National Monument
Dead Horse Ranch
State Park

Clarkdale

Cottonwood

Cornville

Verde River

Verde River

Oak Creek

Creek

134

796

119

89A

260

119

179

Exit 298

Beaver Creek

Montezuma
Castle
National
Monument

Montezuma
Well

Beaver Creek

618

Wet

17

79

260

Camp Verde
Military Reservation
(Abandoned)

Camp Verde

79

17

Statute miles

0   6

Paul Woodward, © 1998 The Countryman Press

BEST TIMES TO FISH THE HATCHES

November 1–January 30
Little Blue-Winged Olive Dun: afternoon, size 20
Trico: morning, sizes 20 to 24

February 1–April 30
Trico: morning and early afternoon, sizes 20 to 24
Black Caddis: afternoon, size 16
Dark Olive Caddis: afternoon, size 12
Little Blue-Winged Olive Dun: afternoon, size 20
Blue-Winged Olive Dun: morning, size 14
Gray Drake: afternoon, size 12

WET BEAVER CREEK

Rating: 5
Access: Good
Seasons: Sp, S, F
Maps: DeLorme pp. 41, 42; Coconino National Forest maps
Positives: Easy access, deep pools and riffles, fishable much of the
   year
Negatives: Warms in summer, heavily fished where it's stocked

As you approach this 20- to 30-foot-wide stream you'll see huge piles of rocks, moved by previous episodes of high water. Towering sycamores and other hardwoods line both banks of the stream. Once you arrive at the Beaver Creek campground, take a look at the stream itself; you'll see plenty of productive riffles, tree falls, and deep pools. You'll get the feeling you're fishing one of a hundred similar streams in the West. You certainly won't think you're just 100 miles north of Phoenix, Arizona.

Wet Beaver flows a few miles south of Sedona and 12 miles southeast of Cottonwood. And the beauty of this trout stream is that you don't have to hike far to reach good fishing. Just a few feet from the parking lot you'll find hatches and, often, rising trout. The Game and Fish Department stocks more than 6000 trout in the area—starting a couple of hundred feet below the bridge and continuing upstream for a mile. If you travel upstream far enough you might even find some holdover fish. Access grows limited up here, though, so plan to hike along the stream if you'd like to fish very far above the bridge.

Wet Beaver receives plenty of snowmelt and discolors quickly. I've been shut out on many March trips because of high, muddy waters. Before making a trip in March or April check with someone in the area. You can usually fish Wet Beaver by mid- to late April.

To reach Wet Beaver from Phoenix, take exit 298 off Interstate 17. Turn right at the end of the exit and proceed for several miles on a blacktop road. Go to the camping site and you'll find a parking lot on your right.

You'll see hatches in early spring on Wet Beaver like the little blue-winged olive dun and some caddis. This stream even holds a limited trico hatch in June and July.

BEST TIMES TO FISH THE HATCHES

March 1–May 31
Little Blue-Winged Olive Dun: afternoon, size 20
Little Black Stonefly: afternoon, size 16
Tan Caddis: evening, size 16

June 1–August 31
Tan Caddis: evening, size 16
Green Caddis: evening, sizes 14 and 16
Trico: morning, size 24
Little Blue-Winged Olive Dun: afternoon, size 20
Olive Caddis: evening, size 16
Little White Mayfly: evening, size 26

OAK CREEK

Rating: 8
Access: Fair (above Sedona); Good (below Sedona)
Seasons: Sp, S, F
Maps: DeLorme p. 42, Coconino National Forest maps
Positives: Spectacular scenery, streambred brown and rainbow trout, great hatches, plenty of productive pools and pocket water
Negatives: Dangerous to fly-fish because of rocks, cliffs, and deep pools; some fishing pressure, weekends often crowded

As Virgil Bradford and I drove along AZ 89A north of Sedona we closely paralleled Oak Creek and the Oak Creek Canyon. *Spectacular—awe inspiring—picturesque*—none of these words does justice to this indescribable piece of landscape, one of nature's greatest accomplishments. None of these adjectives even comes close. The farther north we traveled, the more excited we became to fly-fish this spectacular trout stream.

We finally left our car at one of the parking areas just north of Sliding

CHARLES MECK

Picturesque Oak Creek near Sedona

Rock State Park and looked for a place to get to the water. First we hiked downstream next to the highway, but we saw no reasonable way to access the stream. Then we hiked north and found a steep path heading down to the bottom of the canyon. After sliding the last few feet, we finally arrived at Oak Creek. In front of us was a deep pool with a high cliff on the far side.

On this top-notch trout stream you'll find plenty of productive riffles, deep pools, and pocket water. I immediately checked the water temperature; on a late-February afternoon, it was 42 degrees. Probably few hatches today, I thought—and no rising trout. Not with such a cold water temperature. But no sooner had I replaced the thermometer in my vest than Virgil pointed to several stoneflies struggling to take flight.

We fished for several hundred feet without luck, and then found it impossible to continue upstream. Ahead of us was a high cliff on the far side, a boulder choke on the near side. We had to hike back up the narrow trail to the road, then head upstream to look for another access to the canyon. About 100 yards upstream there was an easier, less dangerous descent to the stream and we continued our barren fishing trip. In a fairly deep but short riffle the dry fly on my tandem sank and I set the hook. A heavy rainbow fought for a minute or two in the cold February water before I landed it.

In Oak Creek's next fairly deep pool, in a feeding lane between two boulders, Virgil saw a trout rise. He pointed it out to me and I cast a foot or two upstream. On the sixth or seventh cast I drifted over the feeding trout it struck—it took my Beadhead and headed deep. It was a heavy fish. Virgil, upstream a hundred feet, reminded me not to horse it. After a five-minute battle I landed and released what looked like a 17-inch holdover brown trout.

Oak Creek holds some good hatches, including the little black stonefly hatch I just mentioned, and an early blue mayfly hatch in late March and early April. You'll see plenty of these insects emerging shortly after noon. You'll also find little blue-winged olives on this stream just about any time of year. Look for them to be especially heavy in April, May, and again in September and early October.

I recently fly-fished in early April on Oak Creek with Rick Thomas, who has fly-fished on this creek for more than 13 years. He and his wife, Perry, know many of its hatches. Rick especially looks forward to the tan caddis hatch in late June and early July. He ties some highly innovative patterns to match both this tan caddis and the many other hatches that the stream holds.

Rick ties commercially and supplies local stores like the Canyon Market, located right on the creek, and John's shop, Arizona Flyfishing, in Tempe.

The day Rick and I fished Oak Creek it was running extremely high from the heavy snows of the past winter. Water temperatures remained in the mid-40s. At 1 PM thousands of "early blues" emerged. Locals say this hatch lasts for almost a month on the stream. No trout rose to this early bonus in the cold water.

Arizona Game and Fish plants trout from the Page Springs Hatchery upstream to Pine Flat Campground (a short distance below Pumphouse Wash and very visible from AZ 89A). The lower end of the stream, from the hatchery upstream to Grasshopper Point, warms considerably in summer, and temperatures in the mid- and high 70s are not uncommon, so the best time to fly-fish this section is in spring, fall, or winter. Here trout fishing is put-and-take. The section from the Page Springs Bridge downstream usually holds some lunker trout. Above Grasshopper Point (about 2 miles above Sedona) you'll find planted and holdover trout, and an occasional wild fish. The state also stocks trout where the West Fork empties into Oak, but upstream from that point the West Fork depends on natural reproduction. In the past few years the Game and Fish Department has annually planted around 70,000 trout in Oak Creek. Stockings usually take place from March through December, but you'll find fish from Sedona upstream all year long.

Take the time to visit the Page Springs Hatchery. Water from the springs remains at 68 degrees year-round. In the Page Springs area Oak Creek ranges from 40 to 60 feet wide. This lower section does warm up during summer. Still, access to this section is much easier than in the canyon. You can reach the lower part of Oak Creek by driving south of Sedona on 89A and taking Forest Road 119 (Cornville Road), then Page Springs Road. Take your time and explore this entire productive watershed.

If you enjoy fly-fishing over rising trout, fishing for holdover trout—even a few streambreds—and experiencing spectacular scenery, then you've got to spend a couple of days fly-fishing Oak Creek. I often have said that there's more to fishing than just catching trout. It's the total experience—and Oak Creek's got it all. Watch your step and enjoy the fishing. Just try to avoid Oak Creek on weekends.

BEST TIMES TO FISH THE HATCHES

February 1–April 30
Little Blue-Winged Olive Dun: afternoon, size 20
Little Black Stonefly: afternoon, sizes 16 and 18
Early Blue *(Baetis tricaudatus)*: afternoon, size 16

May 1–June 30
Little Blue-Winged Olive Dun: afternoon, size 16 or 10
Tan Caddis: evening, size 16
Green Caddis: size 14, evening
Little Golden Stonefly: evening, size 16
Pale Evening Dun: evening, sizes 16 and 18
Trico: morning, size 24

July 1–September 30
Little White Mayfly: evening, size 26
Trico: morning, size 24
Little Blue-Winged Olive Dun; morning, size 18
Yellow Caddis: evening, size 6 or 8

WEST FORK OF OAK CREEK

Rating: 5
Access: Fair
Seasons: Sp, S, F
Maps: DeLorme p. 42, Coconino National Forest maps
Positives: Fewer anglers than the main stem, good pocket water
Negatives: Extremely small

If you like to get off the beaten path and hike in for your fishing, try the West Fork of Oak Creek. You can leave your car at the Call of the Canyon parking area directly across from the stream (a fee is charged for parking). Once you cross Oak Creek there's a trail along the stream. When Rick Thomas fishes the West Fork he usually does so on its lower 3 miles.

The West Fork loses much of its flow in midsummer, and the trout in this small stream get extremely skittish.

The West Fork enters Oak Creek from the west, near the Cave Springs Campground.

BEST TIMES TO FISH THE HATCHES

April 1–May 30
Little Blue-Winged Olive Dun: afternoon, size 20
Blue Dun: afternoon, size 16
Pale Evening Dun: evening, size 16

June 1–September 30
Trico: morning, size 24
Little Blue-Winged Olive Dun: afternoon, size 20

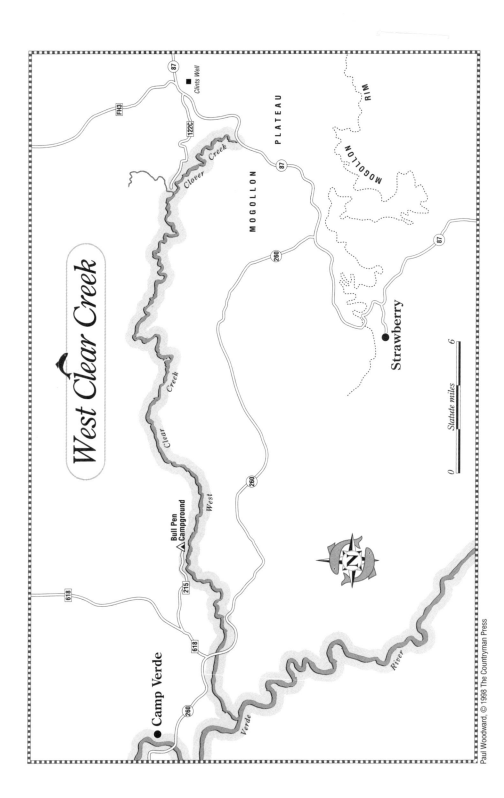

West Clear Creek

Camp Verde

Strawberry

Bull Pen
Campground

MOGOLLON

PLATEAU

MOGOLLON

RIM

Clover Creek

West Clear Creek

Verde River

Clints Well

0   Statute miles   6

Little White Mayfly: evening, size 26
Tan Caddis: evening, size 14 or 16

WEST CLEAR CREEK

Rating: 7
Access: Difficult (upper end); Fair (lower end)
Seasons: Sp, S, F
Maps: DeLorme pp. 42, 50; Coconino National Forest maps
Positives: Plenty of trout, little pressure (except for the campground area), some good hatches
Negatives: Extremely difficult to access in its upper end, lower end warms in summer

When would I ever get into West Clear Creek to fly-fish? For more than two months the stream ran high and off-color. El Niño had played a trick on me, and I'd just about written this stream off. Finally, in early May, I got my opportunity to fish West Clear Creek.

Ryan Gildhaus, an excellent fly-fisher from Cottonwood, had promised to take me into the upper end of this stream. He said that part of the stream, accessed by hiking down a canyon, had a good number of stream-bred trout. In fact, a study by the Arizona Game and Fish Department indicated that more than 22 miles of the upper end holds trout. But hiking in, fishing, and then making the steep hike out of the canyon takes the better part of a day—and I didn't have that much time available. The upper end would have to wait for another day—maybe another year.

I opted to fish the lower end of the stream, about 12 miles east of the town of Camp Verde. The Bull Pen Campground site had plenty of visitors that Saturday afternoon, but few of them were fishing. I headed upstream from the campground to get away from the sounds of civilization. In this area you'll see a stream about 20 to 25 feet wide with some fairly deep pools and productive riffles. It didn't take me long to pick up three planted trout on a Beadhead Pheasant Tail Nymph.

If you enjoy fishing during a hatch you might want to try the trico hatch on West Clear Creek. Look for it to come off in the morning, from late May (even earlier some years) through September. On hot days hatches end shortly after sunrise. On cool, overcast days the same insects might not fall spent on the surface until 9 AM.

Stop in at Culpeppers Bait and Tackle in Cottonwood for the latest information on West Clear Creek and other local streams. Herb and Jim Jackson will go out of their way to help you.

To reach the lower end of the stream take AZ 260 five miles east of Camp Verde. Turn left onto Forest Road (FR) 618, then right onto FR 215—a rutted road that can become greasy in wet weather.

The upper end of West Clear is another story. Take AZ 260 east to AZ 87 north. Turn left onto FR 122C. You can also stop in at the gas station/store in Clints Well to ask for the best way to access the upper creek. Make certain you're in good shape; it's a hike.

BEST TIMES TO FISH THE HATCHES

April 1–May 31
Little Brown Stonefly: afternoon, size 16 or 18
Little Blue-Winged Olive Dun: afternoon, size 20
Quill Gordon: afternoon, size 16
Black Quill: afternoon, size 14

June 1–September 30
Tan Caddis: evening, sizes 14 and 16
Green Caddis: evening, sizes 14 and 16
Pale Evening Dun: evening, size 16
Trico: morning, size 24
Little White Mayfly: evening, size 24 or 26
Little Blue-Winged Olive Dun: afternoon, size 20

5

The Payson-Young Area and the Western Mogollon Rim

Every time I head up the Beeline Highway to Payson from the Phoenix area I am amazed by the transition from desert floor and cactus to high country and pine trees, and, yes, even snow in the winter. This central area of Arizona has much to offer anglers and visitors alike. Many trout streams flow from springs emerging from the Mogollon Rim. Tonto, Horton, Christopher, and Haigler Creeks flow just a few miles from Payson, away from the Rim and south. Heading east toward the Rim on AZ 260 is an experience in itself. The elevation in the Payson area averages around 4500 feet, so you can expect to see some snow in the winter, and the nighttime temperatures at this altitude can get downright low. As you drive toward the Rim you'll often encounter more snow in winter. At the Rim itself you'll find elevations of around 7500 feet and here snow, bad roads, frozen lakes, and cold temperatures are common throughout winter. Streams on the Rim like Chevelon and East Clear usually aren't fishable until April or May. With the relatively low elevations around Payson, though, you can often fish streams like the East Verde River, Tonto, and Christopher Creeks in February and March. And you'll see hatches throughout much of the year. Little black stoneflies cover the waters at midday in February and March.

If you're interested in Arizona history you've got to visit the town of Young—and as a bonus, within a few miles of this old western town you can fish Haigler, Cherry, Spring, and Workman Creeks. How do you get to Young? There's no easy way. If you come from the south you'll travel

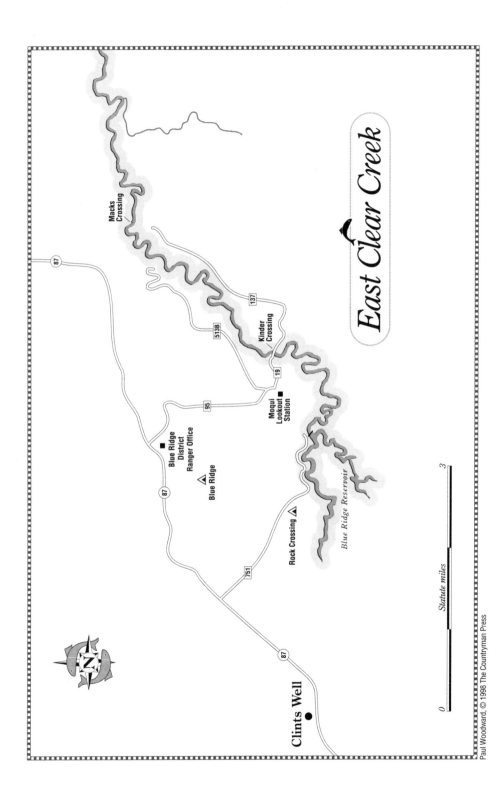

East Clear Creek

Clints Well

Macks Crossing

Blue Ridge District Ranger Office

Blue Ridge

Rock Crossing

Moqui Lookout Station

Kinder Crossing

Blue Ridge Reservoir

87

751

95

513B

137

19

N

0   Statute miles   3

AZ 288, which is 45 miles of dirt. From the north you can drive in from the Mogollon Rim—this time on 20 miles of dirt road. Take AZ 260 east out of Payson and turn right onto the Concord Road (AZ 291). Bear right onto AZ 200, toward Haigler Canyon. This dirt road ends at AZ 288, which will take you south (turn right) to Young.

Tonto, Haigler, and Christopher Creeks have given me many pleasurable fishing days. I remember fly-fishing in early March and having to wade through knee-deep snowdrifts to get to the streams. Once on the streams I saw stoneflies appear and settle on the snow. Even under these adverse conditions I managed to catch a few trout.

What hatches will you see on the streams and rivers of the Payson-Young area? You'll see some not mentioned much in fly-fishing literature, like the dark blue dun *(Thraulodes bicornuta)*. This mayfly, along with the little white mayfly *(Caenis* spp.), trico, and little blue-winged olives, is found on many of the streams of this area.

Don't forget that many of the streams in this area are difficult to reach, so plan your fishing trips accordingly and allow extra time.

EAST CLEAR CREEK

Rating: 7
Access: Difficult
Seasons: Sp, S, F
Maps: DeLorme pp. 43, 50; Coconino National Forest maps
Positives: Some large brown trout, little angling pressure
Negatives: Difficult to access

There's one thing I found out very quickly when I started working with Arizona fly-fishers: They keep a lot of their favorite streams and lakes to themselves. East Clear Creek near Happy Jack, Arizona, is a good example.

I recently talked to Al Correll of Clints Well, Arizona, about some of the lakes and streams in his area. He'll talk for hours about Blue Ridge Reservoir, Knoll Lake, and other local stillwater trout fishing. He'll take you to the Long Valley Service Center in that same little town, where Lynn Ordean will show you rows and rows of photos of trout taken in local lakes. But ask Al about East Clear Creek and he cringes a bit and tells you how difficult it is to fish that "darned stream."

"My heart won't take the hike into that stream anymore." Al says.

But Al also talks of anglers who hike into East Clear Creek and come out with a "lot of big brown trout." East Clear Creek, it seems, is a typical Arizona trout stream—it's not for the faint of heart.

Don't expect to fish this stream too early in the season. If heavy spring snowfalls occur, you can't get here until late April. After El Niño in 1998 roads into East Clear were closed until mid-May. I know because in late April that year I traveled up the Mogollon Rim on AZ 87. Nature had dumped 2 feet of snow on the area and Forest Road (FR) 141 to Jones Crossing was closed. Roads to Kinder and Macks Crossings were also closed with the high snowfall.

But what a spectacular ride!

East Clear Creek holds some good hatches. When you hit a heavy one you can often have a fantastic day matching it over rising trout. Tricos appear in the morning and little white mayflies in the evening in July and August. In April and May and again in September and October you'll also see trout rising to little blue-winged olives in the afternoon. Don't overlook downwings on this stream. In June you'll see little brown stoneflies, tan caddis, and green caddis.

The Happy Jack Lodge is 17 miles from Kinder Crossing on East Clear Creek. Recently I met Matt Carey there. Matt has fished East and West Clear Creeks all his life. He recommends that you walk into the Kinder Crossing area and fish upstream. Matt feels that a lot of the trout stocked in Blue Ridge Reservoir come over the top and stay in the upper few miles of East Clear Creek. He suggests you try this area especially in the latter part of April and early May.

You can reach this productive trout stream off AZ 87 on top of the Rim. Take FR 95 south from AZ 87 to get to Kinder Crossing. You'll find FR 95 about 10 miles north of Clints Well. Turn off AZ 87 and travel about 6 miles on an improved dirt road. Access to the creek below Macks Crossing is on a series of unimproved forest roads.

East Clear flows northeast and empties into the Little Colorado River near Winslow. There's about 30 miles of good fishing. The stream does get low in summer.

BEST TIMES TO FISH THE HATCHES

April 1–May 31
Early Blue or Little Blue-Winged Olive Dun: afternoon, size 16
Little Black Caddis: afternoon, size 16

June 1–September 30
Little Brown Stonefly: evening, size 16
Little White Mayfly: evening, size 26
Pale Evening Dun: evening, size 16
Trico: morning, size 24

Tan Caddis: evening, size 16
Green Caddis: evening, size 16
Little Blue-Winged Olive Dun: afternoon, size 20

EAST VERDE RIVER

Rating: 5
Access: Fair
Seasons: Sp, S, F
Maps: DeLorme p. 50, Tonto National Forest maps
Positives: Easy to reach, stocked heavily, holds some good hatches
Negatives: Extremely limited flow at times, angling pressure

I call the East Verde River a Jekyll-and-Hyde trout stream. Virgil Bradford owned a cabin on this river for several years. He's told me stories about high and low water conditions here; about the time horrendous summer thunderstorms inundated the area; and about the times he saw little if any water flow past his house. Virgil's also told me about the trout he released behind his house.

Some of the water in the East Verde comes (via an aquaduct) from the

The East Verde River near Payson

Blue Ridge Reservoir on top of the Mogollon Rim. When the Phelps Dodge Company operates its mine, Arizona Public Service pumps water into the river; it enters near Washington Park. Historically, a ½-mile section of the river—from the Control Road downriver—runs underground when the water flow lowers in summer.

The state stocks this 20- to 30-foot-wide stream from the Control Road area downriver to a point a few hundred feet below the AZ 87 bridge. Of its lower end, before it enters the Verde River, Mike Weisser of Payson says that he's experienced some of the best smallmouth bass fishing in the state.

To reach the upper end of the East Verde take AZ 87 north from Payson and turn right on Houston Mesa Road. You have to travel about 9 miles on this dirt road before you reach the river, and you'll encounter two water crossings before you reach Control Road. There are several parking areas along Houston Mesa Road. To reach the lower end of the trout-stocking area take AZ 87 north from Payson for a few miles, until you see a bridge crossing the river. Turn left onto a dirt road just before this bridge and park along there.

Beadhead patterns are especially effective on the East Verde. Virgil Bradford often recounts the times he's caught trout on a tandem consisting of a Patriot and a Beadhead Pheasant Tail Nymph. He says that he's caught a lot of trout with the Patriot—and when that doesn't work he catches them on the wet fly, the Beadhead Pheasant Tail.

The East Verde also has some tributaries that hold trout. Dude, Webber (see page 66), and Ellison (see the hatch chart on page 67) hold some trout.

If you fish the river in April or May you'll probably see some little blue-winged olives on the surface in the afternoon. In June and July you'll see pale evening duns appearing in the evening, and tricos in the morning.

BEST TIMES TO FISH THE HATCHES

April 1–May 31
Little Black Stonefly: afternoon, size 16
Little Blue-Winged Olive Dun: afternoon, size 20
Early Brown Stonefly: afternoon, size 14

June 1–August 31
Dark Brown Dun: afternoon, size 14
Pale Evening Dun: evening, size 16
Green Caddis: evening, size 14
Tan Caddis: evening, size 14
Trico: morning, size 24

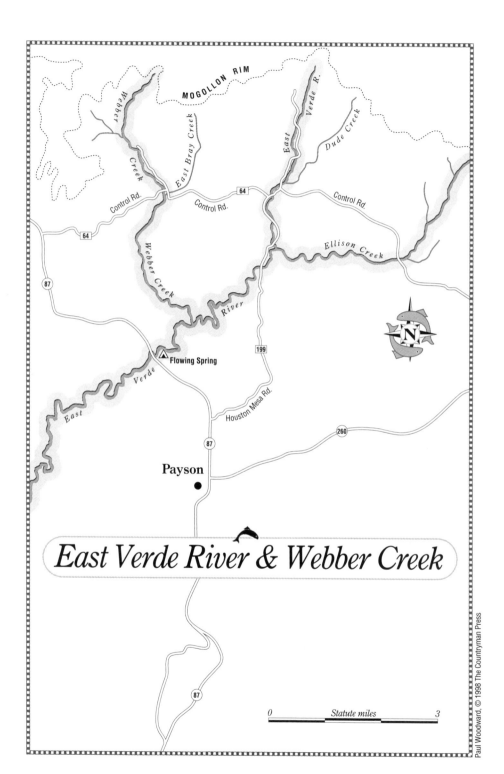

MOGOLLON RIM

Webber Creek

East Bray Creek

East Verde R.

Dude Creek

64

Control Rd.

Control Rd.

Control Rd.

64

64

Webber Creek

Ellison Creek

River

87

199

⛺ Flowing Spring

East Verde

Houston Mesa Rd.

260

87

Payson
●

East Verde River & Webber Creek

N

0   Statute miles   3

Paul Woodward, © 1998 The Countryman Press

Little Blue-Winged Olive Dun: afternoon, size 20
Little White Mayfly: evening, size 24 or 26

September 1–October 30
Trico: morning, size 24
Little Blue-Winged Olive Dun: afternoon, size 20

WEBBER CREEK

Rating: 5
Access: Fair
Seasons: Sp, S, F
Maps: DeLorme p. 50, Tonto National Forest maps
Positives: Not heavily fished, plenty of small pools and pockets
Negatives: Small, limited access, gets extremely low in summer

Schools were closed for the day in Payson. In a cruel April Fool's joke, nature had dumped 10 inches of snow on the town—right on top of the blooming daffodils and blossoming peach trees—and on the very day I planned to fly-fish Webber Creek.

But I headed up Houston Mesa Road just outside Payson anyway, toward the East Verde River, making two river crossings and turning left onto Control Road (FR 64). I then headed west on the improved dirt road for about 6 miles, crossed another stream—Bray Creek—and arrived at Webber Creek. I caught only three small rainbow trout on a Beadhead Pheasant Tail Nymph.

At first glance Webber is small—about 10 to 20 feet wide during much of the fishing season. It has a decent supply of streambred rainbow trout and some respectable hatches. In spring you'll find plenty of little blue-winged olive duns on the water; on midsummer evenings you'll find pale evening duns on the surface; and from July through September you'll even see some tricos emerging in the morning.

You can reach Webber Creek from three directions. First, you can go the way I did, taking Houston Mesa Road just north of Payson, making two water crossings of the East Verde River, and turning left on Control Road. Second, you can take Control Road east from AZ 87; you'll find Control Road about 10 miles north of Payson on your right. This second route normally has no creek crossings. Finally, you can access Webber by taking Control Road from the east at Tonto Village. This is the longest route, but it also allows you to access the upper end of Ellison Creek, which holds some trout. Tonto Village is where AZ 260 and Control Road intersect, east of Payson.

BEST TIMES TO FISH THE HATCHES

April 1–May 31
Little Blue-Winged Olive Dun: afternoon, size 20
Quill Gordon: afternoon, size 16

June 1–September 30
Tan Caddis: evening, size 16
Green Caddis: evening, size 16
Pale Evening Dun: evening, size 16
Little White Mayfly: evening, size 26
Dark Blue Dun: evening, size 14
Trico: morning, size 24
Little Blue-Winged Olive Dun: afternoon, size 20

ELLISON CREEK

BEST TIMES TO FISH THE HATCHES

April 1–May 31
Little Blue-Winged Olive Dun: afternoon, size 20
Little Brown Stonefly: afternoon and evening, size 16

June 1–August 31
Dark Brown Dun: morning, size 14
Trico: morning, size 24 (spotty)
Green Caddis: evening, size 14

TONTO CREEK

Rating: 6
Access: Good (above Kohl's Ranch); Difficult (below Kohl's Ranch)
Seasons: Year-round
Maps: DeLorme pp. 50, 51; Tonto National Forest maps
Positives: Deep pools, some streambred rainbow trout, scenic sections, some good hatches
Negatives: Difficult terrain, some sections difficult or impossible to reach, parts in Hellsgate Canyon impossible to fish, accessible areas heavily fished

On June 25, 1990, a lightning bolt and resulting fire destroyed 24,000 acres of ponderosa pines in the Tonto Basin. The Dude Fire, as most people now call it, turned out to be the worst forest fire in Arizona history. It destroyed much of the timber from the Mogollon Rim down to the Tonto Creek Hatchery, along with one hatchery building; employees saved the rest of the buildings. If you fish Tonto Creek just below the hatchery you'll still see scars from that famous fire.

Mid-February—what a great time to fly-fish in Arizona! But I expected that fishing Tonto Creek at this time—or, to be more specific, fishing Tonto Creek just below Kohl's Ranch in the area locals call Tontozona— would be another story. In the shadows of the pines next to the stream, foot-deep snowbanks still hid much of the ground. And I could hardly expect to see any hatches—not under these conditions! Still, Virgil Bradford and I decided to head up to this stream just north of Payson for a day of fly-fishing. Virgil parked the car just north of Payson on AZ 260 at Kohl's Ranch. We hiked downstream a mile before we decided to fish.

As we hiked Virgil pointed to a couple of deep pools where he had caught a half-dozen trout just a few weeks before, in late November. But things had changed in those few weeks. For one, the water temperature had dropped quite a bit. When I checked it at 10 AM I recorded a 48-degree reading, fairly cool for any hatch or feeding activity. We continued our trek downstream, passing a dozen deep pools and productive-looking riffles. We fished a couple of these but had no luck.

A half mile below Kohl's Ranch Tonto Creek takes on a rugged uninviting look, with deep gorges, sheer cliffs, and boulder chokes along the stream; you must either swim, wade, or hike uphill around these obstacles. On many occasions Virgil and I could only fish 100-yard sections of the stream at a time. After about two hours of acting like a billy goat I asked Virgil if he had had enough. Neither one of us had had a strike.

Still, as we exited the water I noticed a little black stonefly on the snow next to the stream. I looked more closely; there were dozens of these freaks of nature crawling around on the snowbanks. I stopped, took some photos of these downwings, and glanced back toward the stream. Dozens of these insects fluttered on the surface, struggling in the cold air to become airborne. In warmer weather, perhaps the trout might have started rising to this early-season food. Not today.

We hiked back upstream toward our car to fish some of the more accessible water there. Finally, after maybe a couple of hundred casts, I had a strike on Tonto Creek. I landed what looked like a 5-inch streambred rainbow and looked upstream to Virgil. He, too, was landing a small rainbow on a Midge Pupa pattern. In the next 100 yards each of us had a few more strikes and landed a few more trout. Virgil assured me that he had landed and released dozens of small rainbows in this section just two months earlier.

CHARLES MECK

Although the flow in late spring can look scant,
Tonto Creek can still be quite productive.

So what about fly-fishing Tonto at other times of the year? Craig Joseph-son of Syracuse, New York, and I fished the Tontozona area on a warm late-May day several years ago. We headed downstream from AZ 260 toward the Hellsgate Wilderness, because upstream we counted dozens of anglers. Thunderheads above suggested that a severe storm was coming.

When Craig first looked at the scant flow in Tonto he wondered aloud if it could hold any trout. We'd soon find out. We looked again toward the ominous sky as we headed downstream past the Arizona State University practice football field and decided not to hike downstream any farther; we'd fish the first few pools below the practice field. Within a minute Craig had a heavy planted rainbow on a size 16 Beadhead Hare's Ear Nymph. Before I had even begun casting he hooked a second rainbow; this one looked like a wild fish. In this one deep pool we caught a half-dozen trout.

We headed downstream a few hundred feet to the next productive look-ing spot. On his first cast Craig hooked a heavy trout, but it immediately slipped the hook. On his next cast the same trout struck the Beadhead again, and Craig landed a 12-inch rainbow.

Now the sky really darkened and we ran for the car a mile upstream. Just as we reached it hail and heavy rain hit the ground.

Tonto Creek averages 20 to 40 feet wide in the Kohl's Ranch area. It holds many pools over 10 feet deep, some narrow boulder-lined gorges, sheer cliffs, and some productive riffles. If you plan to hike downstream toward the Hellsgate Wilderness Area it might be a better idea to take hiking boots and a backpack, rather than suiting up at your car.

About 2 miles below Kohl's Ranch, Christopher Creek enters Tonto from the northeast. Both streams, along with another tributary, Haigler Creek, hold some streambred trout. Access to the area around Kohl's Ranch is limited because much of the property is private. Respect the owners and access the stream below just below Kohl's Ranch via posted signs. Above AZ 260 access is much easier via Forest Road (FR) 289 to the hatchery. Here you'll find about 4 miles of relatively easy access along the paved road that follows the stream to the hatchery. In this upper area the forest is scarred from the recent fire; the stream is 10 to 15 feet wide.

You'll see a lot of anglers from Tontozona upstream to the hatchery. The easy road access and streamside camping encourage plenty of angling activity.

Tonto Creek begins at several large springs at the base of the Mogollon Rim. The first mile or so of the stream at the hatchery is closed to fishing. Horton Creek enters Tonto about 3 miles downstream from the hatchery. A hiking trail parallels this creek for 4 miles. In this small tributary you'll find streambred brown trout, although Horton suffered severely from the drought in summer 1996, as did other Arizona streams; it will take time for some of them to recover. (See Horton Creek on page 71.) In the upper end of Tonto Creek are a couple of spectacular waterfalls. One of them, Tonto Waterfalls, is just off the road.

You can access the upper end of Tonto Creek off AZ 260 about 15 miles northeast of Payson at Kohl's Ranch. If you're heading up to the Rim, turn left off AZ 260 to reach the creek's upper end; turn right to access the Tontozona Camp area.

The Game and Fish Department stocks trout in the stretch from AZ 260 upstream to the hatchery, just below Kohl's Ranch at Tontozona, and downstream at Bear Flats. A total of about 10 miles of the upper portion of Tonto gets planted trout. Stocking usually begins in April and continues through August.

Tonto Creek holds some great hatches—and they begin early. As early as March you'll see plenty of little black stoneflies, brown stoneflies, and quill gordons. Occasionally you'll find trout as far downstream as Gisela—an Old West town with the spectacular scenery that's worth a trip in itself. This lower area of the stream also holds an unbelievable trico hatch from May through November.

BEST TIMES TO FISH THE HATCHES

February 1–April 30
Little Black Stonefly: afternoon, size 18
Quill Gordon: afternoon, size 16
Early Brown Stonefly: afternoon, size 14
Early Blue or Little Blue-Winged Olive Dun: afternoon, size 16

May 1–June 30
Pale Morning Dun: morning, size 16 (spotty)
Tan Caddis: evening, size 16
Black Quill: evening, size 14
Trico: morning, size 24

July 1–September 30
Tan Caddis: evening, size 16
Green Caddis: evening, size 14
Trico: morning, size 24
Little Blue-Winged Olive Dun: afternoon, size 20

HORTON CREEK

Rating: 4
Access: Fair
Seasons: S, F
Maps: DeLorme p. 51, Tonto National Forest maps
Positives: Easy to reach, scenic, streambred brown trout
Negatives: Plenty of hikers on the trail, suffered from the drought several years ago, very small

Horton Creek has experienced some extremely dry years, and as a result the trout (very spooky streambred browns) and insects it holds suffered considerably. Some anglers feel the best time to try Horton Creek is in late March or early April, before the hordes of hikers arrive. The farther upstream you fish on this 4-mile-long stream, the better your chances of success.

Recently Virgil Bradford and I fly-fished this 10-foot-wide stream in late March. We hiked only ½ mile upstream because of foot-deep snowdrifts along the bank. With water temperatures in the low 40s we didn't catch even one trout. Still, they are there.

Don't expect to see much in the way of hatches, which are recovering from the low water flow of a few years ago. Even little brown stoneflies

Horton Creek, a tributary to Tonto Creek, holds some streambred brown trout.

and blue-winged olives, common Arizona hatches, are scarce.

To reach Horton, turn north off AZ 260 at Kohl's Ranch and travel 1 mile. You'll see a bridge crossing Tonto Creek. There's a parking lot on the other side of the bridge for those hiking the Horton Creek Trail (#285), which in turn takes you 4 miles upstream to Horton Spring, the source of Horton Creek.

If you enjoy hiking, beautiful scenery, fishing very small streams with some brush, and catching an occasional wild trout—you'll enjoy fishing Horton Creek.

BEST TIMES TO FISH THE HATCHES

April 1–June 30
Little Blue-Winged Olive Dun: afternoon, sizes 20 to 24
Little Brown Stonefly: afternoon, size 18

July 1–September 30
Little Blue-Winged Olive Dun: afternoon, size 20

CHRISTOPHER CREEK

Rating: 5
Access: Fair
Seasons: S, F
Maps: DeLorme p. 51, Tonto National Forest maps
Positives: If you like to explore, here's the place to do it; relatively easy to reach
Negatives: Rough terrain in places, few access points

On a late-March afternoon I hiked into the Christopher Creek Campground. I *had* to hike, because the road into this particular tourist spot was closed until May 1. I continued ½ mile upstream from the campground and sat on a huge ledge that led to the stream. As I stared at the swollen, muddy water I saw a great hatch of little black stoneflies emerge for more than an hour. No trout rose to this plentiful supply of food because of the snowmelt-swollen waters.

Christopher Creek holds plenty of great hiding spots for trout. You'll find good-sized, boulder-choked pools; deep pockets formed by smaller boulders and ledges; and some deep runs. Watch your step when you fish this 10- to 20-foot-wide-stream. Rocks of various sizes are scattered along the banks, and larger boulders and ledges prevent easy access to many parts of the stream.

The state stocks essentially three spots on Christopher; the campground site (where you'll find lots of angling pressure); the Scout Ranch site; and the See Canyon area. You should enjoy fly-fishing the upper area of the creek, in the See Canyon. To reach Christopher Creek, drive northeast on AZ 260 from Payson. The campground is near the town of Christopher Creek; from there FR 284 goes north to See Canyon. Scout Ranch is a couple of miles southeast of the campground.

This section of Christopher Creek holds a good little brown stonefly hatch in April.

CHARLES MECK

Christopher, like all the tributaries of Tonto Creek, holds a great little blue-winged olive dun hatch in spring and again in fall. On its lower end, where it enters Tonto Creek, you can match tricos from June through September.

BEST TIMES TO FISH THE HATCHES

March 10–May 31
Little Black Stonefly: afternoon, size 16
Early Blue or Little Blue-Winged Olive Dun: afternoon, size 16
Pale Morning Dun: morning, size 16

June 1–September 30
Tan Caddis: evening, size 14
Trico: morning, size 24
Little Yellow Stonefly: evening, size 16
Little Blue-Winged Olive Dun: afternoon, size 20

HAIGLER CREEK

Rating: 6
Access: Fair
Seasons: Sp, S, F
Maps: DeLorme p. 51, Tonto National Forest maps
Positives: Scenic stream, brown trout in the upper reaches
Negatives: Heavy angling pressure where the stream is stocked, a four-wheel-drive vehicle is needed for access in spring

Plenty of Arizona history is associated with Haigler Creek, Pleasant Valley, and the cowboy town of Young. In 1879 the Tewksbury brothers moved into Pleasant Valley to operate a cattle ranch. Several years later the Graham brothers settled just a couple of miles away. Thus began a family feud that came to include cattle rustling, killings, and almost continuous conflict between the two families for nearly a decade. Rustic Young is today a town almost in a time warp, and the area around it classic Old West. Stop in the local saloon for a taste of history; they'll be delighted to talk to you. But they don't want you to move here. Both the northern and southern entrances to this town are gravel and most residents want to keep them that way.

Fred Brauburger and I fished Haigler Creek in late March. Fred lives in Scottsdale, Arizona, and has fly-fished all over the West. He's spent weeks on the Dolores River in Colorado, days on New Mexico's San Juan, and

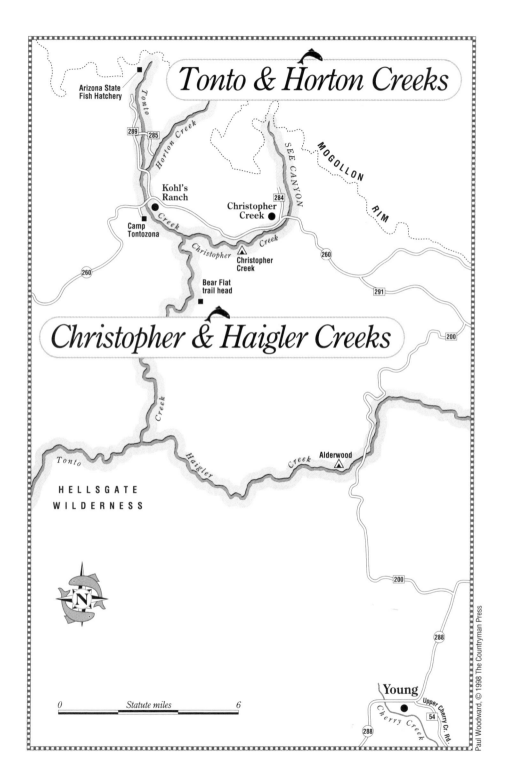

Tonto & Horton Creeks

Arizona State
Fish Hatchery

Tonto

289 285

Horton Creek

Kohl's
Ranch

Creek

Camp
Tontozona

Christopher
Creek

284

SEE CANYON

MOGOLLON RIM

Christopher   *Creek*

Christopher
Creek

260

260

291

Bear Flat
trail head

Christopher & Haigler Creeks

200

Creek

Haigler   *Creek*

Alderwood

200

Tonto

HELLSGATE
WILDERNESS

N

288

Young

Upper Cherry Cr. Rd.

54

Cherry Creek

288

0   Statute miles   6

weeks on rivers in Montana searching for lunker trout. Fred's a natural fly-fisher. Give him a fly-rod and a few Beadheads, put him on a good stream, and he'll catch trout. On the dozens of occasions I've fly-fished with him I've seen him outfish every angler on the stream. Fred often uses a tandem made up of a Patriot dry fly and a gray Beadhead. If that doesn't work he resorts to two Beadheads—one brown, one gray. In any event, when Fred's not off fly-fishing the great rivers of Montana or Colorado, you'll often see him here, on one of the trout streams on or near Arizona's Mogollon Rim. Haigler Creek is among Fred's favorites.

To reach Haigler Creek from Young, drive a few miles north on AZ 288 and turn left onto Forest Road (FR) 200, Chamberlain Road. Travel about 8 miles on improved dirt until you reach a low-water crossing for Haigler Creek. Above the crossing you'll see some camping sites and national forest land. A half mile below it you'll see some posted private land. Please respect private property here, and elsewhere.

You can also reach the stream by turning south off AZ 260 near Christopher Creek. Take Colcord Road (FR 291), then turn right onto Chamberlain Road (FR 200) and proceed to the stream. Don't attempt to travel the upper end of Chamberlain Road from December through March.

The state stocks the stream heavily where FR 200 crosses, and you'll consequently find plenty of angling pressure in this area. Haigler Creek runs from 15 to 20 feet wide and holds plenty of 3- and 4-foot-deep pools and productive riffles. It can be easily negotiated with hipboots.

You'll find some good hatches on Haigler, especially from April through June. The stream holds some little blue-winged olives that appear much of the season. Its lower end holds a great trico hatch that appears every morning throughout summer. Hike upstream or downstream to get away from angling pressure and you'll find some streambred brown trout.

Haigler Creek enters the Hellsgate Wilderness 8 miles downstream from FR 200.

BEST TIMES TO FISH THE HATCHES

April 1–May 31
Early Blue or Little Blue-Winged Olive Dun: afternoon, size 16

June 1–September 30
Dark Blue Dun: evening, size 16
Pale Evening Dun, evening, size 16
Trico: morning, size 24
Little White Mayfly: evening, size 26

Haigler Creek holds some caddisfly hatches.

Tan Caddis: evening, size 14
Green Caddis: evening, size 14
Little Blue-Winged Olive Dun: afternoon, size 20

CANYON CREEK

[handwritten annotation: House to 260 turn off - 70 miles / Turnoff to 288 turn - 32 miles / 288 turn to CC turn - 3 miles / CC turn to lower CC - 6 miles]

Rating: 8
Access: Fair
Seasons: Sp, S, F
Maps: DeLorme p. 51, Tonto National Forest maps
Regulations: Artificial lures and flies only from OW Bridge to White
  Mountain Apache Reservation in Gila County
Positives: Nice wild browns, close to metro area, abundant wildlife,
  campgrounds nearby
Negatives: Catch-and-release area needs better policing

Canyon Creek is one of Arizona's most successful trout stories. This is the Mogollon Rim area's best stream—indeed, it's used by more anglers than any other stream here. It begins at the base of the Rim and flows south for over 50 miles, mostly on the White Mountain Apache Reservation, eventually emptying into the Salt River. The first 5.8 miles are in the Tonto National Forest; this is the water I'll be discussing.

The stream has had its share of problems from both Mother Nature and man. The monsoon rains that strike Arizona during summer months can unload tremendous amounts of water in a short period of time. In 1984, the flood resulting from one of these storms scoured Canyon Creek, filling in its pools with silt and tearing away much of the streamside vegetation. Huge cottonwoods that had shaded the water and kept it cool were torn from their roots and deposited in the channels or left decaying on the banks. Cattle were then allowed to graze the area, destroying the stream banks and fouling the water. The quality of the fishing declined. Clearly something had to be done to correct its problems or Canyon Creek was going to cease to be a trout fishery.

Through the efforts of Trout Unlimited and the National Forest Service, the Canyon Creek Aquatic Habitat Improvement Operational Plan was initiated in 1986. This called for the stream to be managed as a blue-ribbon fishery; its goal was a self-sustaining brown trout and rainbow fishery by 1991. With the help of two local clubs, the Desert Flycasters and Arizona Flycasters, the stream was renovated. Two-ton logs were cut on site and strategically placed in the stream bank to stop erosion during the spring floods. One-ton boulders were placed in the stream to provide cover

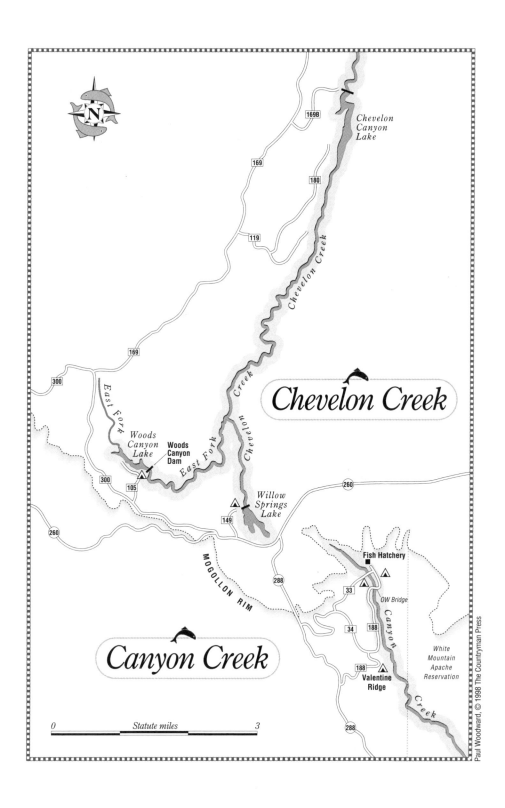

N

169B

Chevelon
Canyon
Lake

169

180

119

Chevelon Creek

169

300

East Fork

Chevelon Creek

🐟 *Chevelon Creek*

Woods
Canyon
Lake

Woods
Canyon
Dam

East Fork

Chevelon Creek

300

105

Willow
Springs
Lake

149

260

260

MOGOLLON RIM

288

Fish Hatchery

33

OW Bridge

Canyon Creek

34

188

🐟 *Canyon Creek*

188

Valentine
Ridge

White
Mountain
Apache
Reservation

288

Creek

0   Statute miles   3

Paul Woodward, © 1998 The Countryman Press

and help secure the logs during high water. Protective cover for the trout was built by placing the butt ends of logs in the bank; lashing them together with heavy screening kept them in place. Dirt was then placed on the cover and willows planted to bind the soil—which just a few years later provided the shade needed to keep the creek cool during the hot summer months. To this day, you can't tell that any work was ever done here unless you look for it.

The Arizona Boys Ranch took on the ambitious job of building 3½ miles of fencing to keep cattle out of the streambed. Easy-access gates were strategically placed along the fence to allow anglers in and keep cattle out. This was undoubtedly the most beneficial addition to Canyon Creek. Without the livestock tearing up the area, watercress began to grow in the stream. Young willows sprouted up everywhere, too, and reduced the stream's summer temperature by 5 degrees—to 69. Without this fencing all the stream's renovations would have gone for naught.

Brown trout soon began reproducing well in the stream; by 1989 an estimated 5000 browns (some up to 7 pounds) were residing in Canyon Creek. The rainbows didn't fare as well, however, so their populations were supplemented with annual stockings of 400 to 600 six-inch fish.

New regulations were passed in 1990 to allow the harvest of two trout of any species with a minimum size of 12 inches. These regulations were intended to increase angler use. They succeeded. Indeed, because the policing of the lure-and-fly area was so poor, you could consistently find bait jars and worm containers littering the banks of the stream.

In January 1993, Mother Nature took control again. A major flood devastated the stream. Some of the renovation work held and is still in place; it surely helped minimize bank erosion. Many of the large cottonwoods and willows along the stream were uprooted and deposited in the streambed. Some of the large boulders were pushed downstream and created new natural cover and portions of the channel were changed, creating new pools and runs. It was a good example of how powerful the forces of nature can be.

The stream is in very good condition today and is supporting a good population of naturally reproducing browns. Rainbows are still not reproducing; they're stocked at the rate of around 250 a week during the fishing season. The stream is now divided into two separate regulation categories. From the OW Bridge upstream to the hatchery, four trout of any size can be taken with bait. From the OW Bridge downstream to the Apache Indian Reservation, the water is catch-and-release with lure and fly only.

Canyon Creek has a good population of mayflies, mostly *Baetis* and *Heptagenia* spp., plus *Hydropsyche* caddis. Terrestrials work well on the

RON DUNGAN

Falls at Canyon Creek

stream also. In the summer months it's a great hopper stream: Beetles and ants always pick up a few fish, and when they're hatching cicadas can be exciting to fish, especially right along the logs or undercut banks where you know a brown is waiting for a tasty morsel to come drifting by.

I fished this section with Wes Nakata and Dick Roberts of Desert Fly-casters in April 1998. The stream was still high and a little off-color. Although the water temperature was a chilly 44 degrees, and there was little insect activity, we managed to catch a few browns and rainbows on heavily weighted Beadhead Buggers. Dick landed a nice, chunky 15-inch brown with a well-placed cast at the end of a root wad. Wes picked some up with his soft-hackle emerger later in the day, after the sun had warmed the water somewhat. After the El Niño winter of 1997–98, there will surely be plenty of water in this stream, making it one of the better places to try your luck for a nice brown trout.

Canyon Creek is a nice day trip from Phoenix or Tucson, and there are good campgrounds in the area. You can hear turkeys gobbling in spring and big bull elk bugling in fall. More than once, I have seen big bulls come out at dusk to graze in the meadows around the bottom section. Reach the creek by taking AZ 260 east from Payson. Head up the Mogollon Rim until you hit AZ 288 south, a well-maintained gravel road that heads down to Young. Follow the well marked signs to Canyon Creek, about 5 miles altogether.

BEST TIMES TO FISH THE HATCHES

April 1–May 31
Early Blue or Little Blue-Winged Olive Dun: afternoon, size 16
Quill Gordon: afternoon, size 16

June 1–September 30
Pale Evening Dun: evening, size 16
Trico: morning, size 24 (spotty)
Tan Caddis: evening, size 14 or 16
Green Caddis: evening, size 14

CHEVELON CREEK

Rating: 5
Access: Difficult
Seasons: Sp, S, F
Maps: DeLorme p. 51, Tonto National Forest maps
Positives: Big browns, secluded, scenic
Negatives: Tough to fish in summer months, access is difficult

Chevelon is one of the best Arizona streams for big brown trout. Located at the bottom of Chevelon Canyon, it's formed by the junction of Woods Canyon Creek and Willow Springs Creek. The creeks flow approximately 3 miles below the lakes before they join to form Chevelon. From the beginning of Chevelon Creek downstream to Chevelon Canyon Lake is about 10½ miles—a rough 10½ miles. This is rugged, rather remote country, and odds are you won't have any company if you decide to negotiate the full length of the stream down to Chevelon Lake.

Chevelon Creek is predominantly brown trout water, with some rainbows mixed in. The stream is vulnerable to the weather—during dry spells it can suffer from low water, and after prolonged dry spells sections will actually get so low that the streambed is exposed. Water temperatures reach intolerable heights and fishing suffers. This is one reason why the more temperature-tolerant brown trout is surviving in the stream—along with speckled dace and crayfish, which serve as the two main food sources for the predacious browns.

Chevelon Creek offers its best fishing during early spring after the roads are open and the banks are full from the melting winter snows. With the spring runoff in full force, Chevelon will also get a run of trout from the lake below, so early spring can also be the best time to fish upstream from the lake. Depending on how early the roads open and the forest service allows access to the lake, you can catch some nice rainbows coming upstream to spawn. The browns follow the rainbows to feed on their eggs and are susceptible to egg patterns and Egg-Sucking Leeches at this time. I usually fish a chestnut-colored Sparkle Bugger, sometimes with an egg in front; I think the browns take it for an egg-stealing crayfish. Cast up tight against the shore, because the browns tend to hit the shorelines early in search of the year's first crayfish hatch.

Fish Chevelon's deeper pools during the warmer periods of the season. If you're lucky enough to be camping here, try night fishing when the bigger browns feel more comfortable and are out feeding on crayfish and dace. When there is ample water, fall fishing for spawning browns can be awesome.

Keeping your fly close to the bank is a good tactic on Chevelon all year long. In early morning the browns and rainbows are cruising for crayfish that have come in to feed during the night. When it gets warmer and the terrestrials are out in force a big hopper splatted hard on the water works well; fish a cicada the same way when you hear these insects' distinct buzzing noise in the trees. You don't have to be afraid of spooking these fish with a cast that lands too hard on the water. The loud *splat* of a big fly cast hard on the water will actually attract these fish, and they won't gently sip it in when they get to it, either. This is fun fishing and the aggressive takes are a major part of it. Chevelon also has decent numbers of *Baetis* mayflies and green caddis. Afternoons and evenings can see good hatches of both, making for some nice dry-fly fishing.

Chevelon can be accessed from either side of the canyon by using designated trails down the canyon walls. The western side of the canyon is the most commonly used and is accessed by taking AZ 260 up the Rim from Payson. About 45 minutes outside of Payson, look for Forest Road (FR) 300. Turn off 260 and take FR 300 to FR 169. Head north on 169 to FR 119, which dead-ends above the canyon rim. From there you go straight down into the canyon and through some of the prettiest country in the state. If the fish cooperate you'll have a great memory of a huge brown to go along with the guaranteed memory of your long hike out.

BEST TIMES TO FISH THE HATCHES

April 1–May 31
Little Blue-Winged Olive Dun: afternoon, size 20

Flowering cacti along Canyon Creek

June 1–September 30
Black Quill: afternoon, size 16
Pale Evening Dun: evening, size 16
Green Caddis: evening, size 14
Little Brown Stonefly: evening, size 16

CHERRY CREEK

Rating: 5
Access: Fair
Seasons: Sp, S, F
Maps: DeLorme p. 51, Tonto National Forest maps
Positives: Little angling pressure, brown trout in lower end
Negatives: Much of stream is difficult to access

Fred Brauburger and I traveled about 10 miles on a dirt, rutted road to Cherry Creek. As we drove along its lower end, still in desert country, we wondered aloud how good this stream would be if the state used it as part of their winter stocking program. The lower end of Cherry Creek is only a few miles east of Roosevelt Lake. To reach the upper (northern) part of Cherry, where you'll find trout all year long, take AZ 288 to Young.

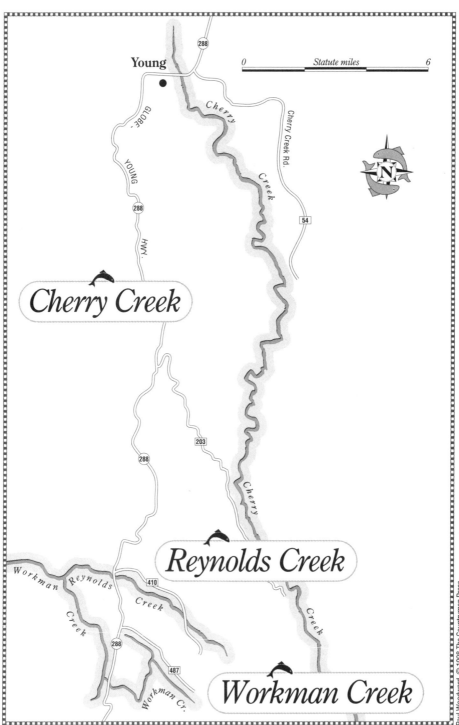

Young

0 Statute miles 6

288

Cherry

Creek

Cherry Creek Rd.

GLOBE-

YOUNG

288

HWY.

54

N

Cherry Creek

203

288

Cherry

Reynolds Creek

Workman

Reynolds

410

Creek

Creek

Creek

288

Workman Creek

487

Workman Cr.

Although there's about 45 miles of gravel, AZ 288 takes you through some of Arizona's most breathtaking scenery. At one point about 15 miles north of Roosevelt Lake, you go from desert to heavy forest—within 100 feet!

To get to the stream take AZ 288 just beyond Young, then turn right onto Upper Cherry Creek Road. (If you've driven into Young from the north, this will be a left turn.) Just ½ mile downstream you'll see the first water crossing. Head south on this gravel road.

Cherry Creek holds some great hatches, including emerging tricos just about every summer morning. This diminutive hatch, however, is much heavier on nearby Haigler Creek. Cherry also holds some fairly respectable caddis hatches.

In the Young area Cherry Creek averages 20 to 30 feet wide. Ten miles below Young, the stream becomes difficult to access.

BEST TIMES TO FISH THE HATCHES

April 1–May 31
Little Blue-Winged Olive Dun: afternoon, size 20
Blue Dun: afternoon, size 16

June 1–September 30
Tan Caddis: evening, size 14
Trico: morning, size 24
Little White Mayfly: evening, sizes 24 and 26
Green Caddis: evening, sizes 14 and 16
Little Blue-Winged Olive Dun: afternoon, size 20

REYNOLDS CREEK

Rating: 5
Access: Fair
Seasons: Sp, S, F
Maps: DeLorme p. 51, Tonto National Forest maps
Positives: Scenic stream with little angling pressure, some good hatches
Negatives: Extremely small stream, gets very low in summer

The El Niño of 1997–98 hit Arizona with a violence few people expected. In the Valley of the Sun precipitation averages 7 inches a year, but by the end of March '98 the area had received well more than half of that amount. Flagstaff and Greer, too, had received well over 100 percent of their average annual snowfall. Flagstaff had its heaviest one-day snowfall

A view of the Mogollon Rim just south of the East Verde River

ever near the end of March. (Meanwhile my summer home, Pennsylvania, was seeing a temperature of 85 degrees!)

This excess precipitation and the cool temperatures had set me back in my quest to fish more than 50 trout streams across the state. Even small streams were running high and muddy in late March, and the snowfall prevented me from reaching some of the waters I wanted to fly-fish. Haigler, Tonto, and Christopher Creeks, along with others around the Payson-Young area, all ran high and off-color.

Fred Brauburger and I left Haigler Creek after a half hour one late-March day because of this high, off-color water. We headed south from the cowboy town of Young on AZ 288 for about 15 miles until we crossed a small stream, Reynolds Creek. Reynolds *is* small—you can jump across it at many spots. But when larger streams are running high or off-color, try this small gem. It begins about 4 miles above AZ 288, at Knoles Hole Spring, at 7200 feet.

Reynolds gets extremely low in the summer, and its rainbow trout are skittish. Still, its fishing is worth the trip on the gravel road. Be careful on wet days—the road gets very slick.

Despite its size Reynolds Creek holds a good population of stoneflies. Carry plenty of downwings and stonefly nymphs with you to this scenic little stream.

BEST TIMES TO FISH THE HATCHES

April 1–May 31
Little Blue-Winged Olive Dun: afternoon, size 20
Little Brown Stonefly: afternoon, size 16 or 18

June 1–September 30
Pale Evening Dun: evening, size 16
Little Yellow Stonefly: afternoon and evening, size 16
Black Quill: morning, size 14
Trico: morning, size 24
Tan Caddis: evening, size 16
Brown Caddis: evening, size 14 and 16
Yellow Caddis: evening, size 14

WORKMAN CREEK

Rating: 5
Access: Fair
Seasons: S, F
Maps: DeLorme p. 51, Tonto National Forest maps
Positives: Spectacular small stream, great scenery, some great
hatches, great early-season stonefly hatch
Negatives: Extremely low in summer

If you've never traveled north on AZ 288 to the town of Young, you're in for an exciting, breathtaking trip. The route, an improved gravel road, begins in the low-desert country around Roosevelt Lake. From there you travel up a winding road out of cactus country into mountains filled with ponderosa pines and elevations of 6000 to 7000 feet, where air temperatures remain in the comfortable zone. About 15 miles up AZ 288 you'll cross scenic little Workman Creek. Forest Road (FR) 487 leaves AZ 288 on your right and parallels the stream's north bank.

Workman Creek flows through heavily forested land. It begins about 5 miles above the road as a spring at 7050 feet. From this spring to AZ 288 it drops almost 2000 feet. Just above the highway you'll see a 10- to 15-foot-wide fast-flowing stream with many 2- to 3-foot pools. If I didn't know any better I'd swear this was a small mountain stream in Montana or Pennsylvania. Don't overlook this small stream below the road.

Even though it's small Workman Creek holds some great hatches; you'll even find some tricos here from late June through September. Carry plenty of Blue Quills in size 18 with you when you fly-fish this small stream; the hatch can be fairly heavy here. Also carry plenty of downwings. Work-man holds a good hatch of little brown stoneflies that appear in the after-noon in April.

BEST TIMES TO FISH THE HATCHES

April 1–May 31
Little Brown Stonefly: afternoon, size 16 or 18
Little Blue-Winged Olive Dun: afternoon, size 20
Blue Quill: morning, size 18
Tan Caddis: evening, size 14 or 16

June 1–September 30
Pale Evening Dun: evening, size 16
Blue Quill: morning, size 18
Trico: morning, size 24
Little Yellow Stonefly: evening, size 16

6

Apache Country

Craig Josephson of Syracuse, New York, and I first fly-fished this country almost a decade ago. We hit the North Fork of the White River at Ditch Camp and at the Alchesay Hatchery in Whiteriver. We experienced a great tan caddis hatch on the North Fork at the town of Whitewater and saw trout rising to the egg layers. We had unbelievable success on Lofer Cienega Run, Big Bonito Creek, and the East Fork of the White River. We fished Sunrise Lake when thousands of speckle-winged duns emerged and dozens of trout rose to the stragglers. What a week of fishing—and it all happened on the White Mountain Apache Reservation. We caught native Apache trout on some of the smaller streams on the reservation, heavy browns on the North Fork and the East Fork of the White River, and plenty of browns on Cibecue Creek.

For the most part you can expect to access Apache country streams in spring, summer, and fall. Winter is no time to be traveling some of the back roads in the reservation. Still, lower waters—the East Fork of the White River, the lower North Fork of the White River just above Whitewater, Cibeceue Creek in Cibecue, and Diamond Creek—can usually be accessed much of winter. However, these streams are stocked only during the spring and summer months. Check local conditions and rules for travel on reservation roads.

The US Fish and Wildlife Service stocks five streams and rivers and 16 lakes on the reservation. Many of these waters receive five or six stockings each spring and summer. Of the moving trout waters, the North Fork of the White River receives the largest number of trout. Authorities stock this river from April through September. The reservation also stocks the

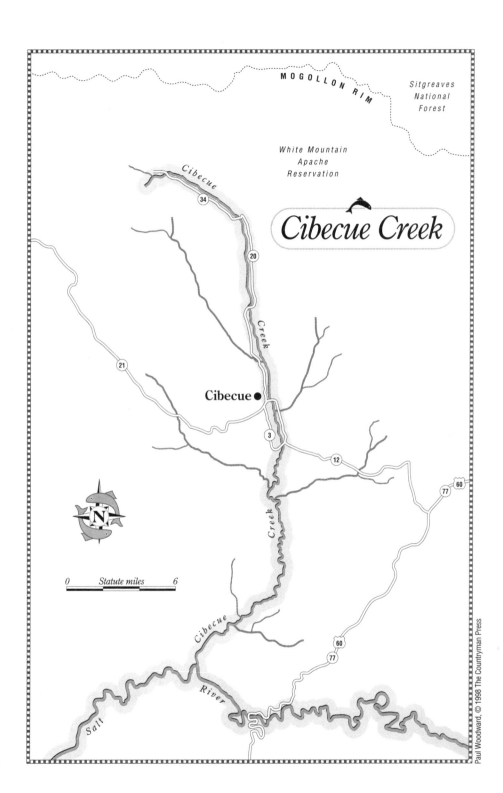

MOGOLLON RIM

Sitgreaves National Forest

White Mountain Apache Reservation

Cibecue

34

20

Cibecue Creek

Creek

21

Cibecue •

3

12

77 60

N

0 Statute miles 6

Cibecue

60 77

River

Salt

East Fork of the White River plus Cibecue, Paradise, and Diamond Creeks, planting Apache trout in the streams and rainbow, Apache, brown, and brook trout in the lakes. The White Mountain Apache tribe should be commended for its management of the reservation's trout streams.

Make certain you obtain the proper permits for entering this scenic, isolated country. You can get information regarding tribal permits by calling the White Mountain Apache Tribal Game and Fish at 520-338-4385 or writing to PO Box 220, Whitewater, AZ 85941. A daily fishing permit costs $5; an annual permit, $80; and a summer permit, $50.

And if you plan to travel on some of the reservation's dirt roads, remember several important items. First, many of the roads on the reservation are poorly marked; trying to find your way from point A to point B can be frustrating. Second, some of the gravel roads are in less-than-ideal condition. Many require four-wheel drive. Finally, remember when you travel to streams like Big Bonito and Lofer Cienega Creeks that you're 20 to 30 miles from the nearest town.

Apache country has plenty to offer the angler and the visitor. I'll examine some of the better trout streams in the area.

[handwritten: We (Chris Sommer, Ryan Mahoney, Mike Leed and I) camped at Cibecue Creek at the end of April. The weather was nice but what an incredibly dirty and trashy place. The Apaches do not take care of this land. In fact, they appear to make an effort to litter. We found a beautiful camp spot and after filling up a trash bag, we had ourselves a nice spot. As far as fishing, none of us had any luck. It must be said that the precipitation for the 99-00 winter was sparse so the water was low and the browns skittish.]

CIBECUE CREEK

Rating: 6

Access: Good

Seasons: Year-round

Maps: DeLorme p. 51, White Mountain Apache maps

Regulations: Tribal permit required

Positives: Little fishing pressure, some good-sized brown trout, relatively easy to fly-fish, good hatches

Negatives: Somewhat difficult to find, small stream, lower end warms in summer

It was April 15 and I was headed to Cibecue Creek, located halfway between Globe and Show Low along AZ 77/US 60. As I turned left off US 60 onto Indian Route 12 a heavy snow squall appeared. Within minutes the road was snow covered. Then it appeared in front of me—Cibecue Creek.

It doesn't look like much of a trout stream. But it does have fairly easy access—that is, if you can find your way on Indian Route 12 to the town of Cibecue, then upstream on Indian Route 20 to Route 34. Once you're there you'll find a 15- to 20-foot-wide, meadowlike stream flowing from the north.

[handwritten: Other books mention White Spring and that the 1st 100 yrds of it hold the majority of the fish. This is difficult to believe considering its small size (2-5 feet wide).]

A view of the North Fork of the White River from the road into Hawley Lake

Cibecue (sometimes spelled differently) flows through Apache country, so make certain you've purchased a tribal permit at the general store in Salt River Canyon before you fly-fish. Try to fish several miles above the town. Here you'll find a stream about 10 to 15 feet wide with brush-covered banks that make fly-casting difficult. As you travel upstream you'll see a tributary, Salt Creek, entering from the left. Try Cibecue just above this confluence. There's little angling pressure and plenty of streambred browns and planted Apache trout. You'll also find heavy brown trout in this area. The tribe plants Apache trout in the stream from April through August.

About 4 miles upstream on Indian Route 34 the road changes from blacktop to gravel, and here it quickly becomes rutted in wet weather. The farther upstream you travel, though, the better your chances to catch trout. The area recently suffered from a forest fire and the stream now tends to discolor rapidly after rainfall or heavy snowmelt.

What about hatches? Take one look at the stream and you'll know that Cibecue hosts a good little blue-winged olive dun hatch in April and again in September. But fish Cibecue in the morning from June through September and you'll see plenty of trico spinners falling on the water. Match this diminutive hatch with a size 20 short-shanked Trico pattern and you'll catch trout.

BEST TIMES TO FISH THE HATCHES

March 1–May 31
Little Blue-Winged Olive Dun: afternoon, size 20

June 1–August 31
Pale Evening Dun: evening, size 16
Green Caddis: afternoon, size 14
Trico: morning, size 24
Little White Mayfly: evening, size 26

September 1–October 30
Trico: morning, size 24
Little Blue-Winged Olive Dun: afternoon, size 20

NORTH FORK OF THE WHITE RIVER

Rating: 7
Access: Fair
Seasons: Year-round
Maps: DeLorme p. 52, 53; White Mountain Apache maps
Regulations: Catch-and-release waters in the Ditch Camp area;
    tribal permit required
Positives: Spectacular scenery, little development, some good
    hatches, isolated areas, streambred brown trout in the upper area
Negatives: Lower end is put-and-take, heavy fishing pressure in the
    Whiteriver area

Every time I begin a talk about western fly-fishing I start with a question-and-answer period. I show several slides of rivers of the United States and ask the audience where each is located. I always include a slide of the Ditch Camp area of North Fork of the White River. When I ask the group where they'll find this river, invariably someone blurts out: "Wyoming, Montana, or Colorado." They're dumbfounded when I finally tell them this river is in Arizona. The North Fork is the kind of typical Western trout river you'd expect to see in the West but—for most anglers—not in Arizona.

A few years ago Craig Josephson and I ended a fantastic weeklong fishing trip to the White Mountains by fly-fishing for two hours on the North Fork of the White River. At Ditch Camp we caught a dozen brown trout from 6 to 12 inches long. We hiked upriver more than a mile, too, and caught more trout in the many pools and riffles on this section of the river. (Ditch Camp is a catch-and-release area 3 miles long. It begins where

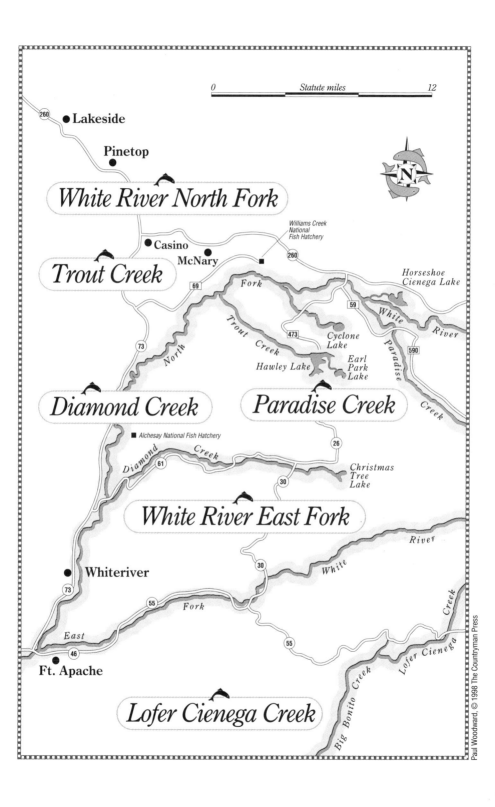

0   Statute miles   12

● Lakeside

Pinetop
●

White River North Fork

Williams Creek
National
Fish Hatchery

● Casino
McNary ●

Trout Creek

Horseshoe
Cienega Lake

Fork

Trout Creek

North

White River

Cyclone
Lake

Earl
Park
Lake

Hawley Lake

Paradise

Creek

Diamond Creek

Paradise Creek

■ Alchesay National Fish Hatchery

Diamond Creek

Christmas
Tree
Lake

White River East Fork

River

White

● Whiteriver

Fork

East Fork

White

Lofer Cienega Creek

● Ft. Apache

Lofer Cienega Creek

Big Bonito Creek

Paul Woodward, © 1998 The Countryman Press

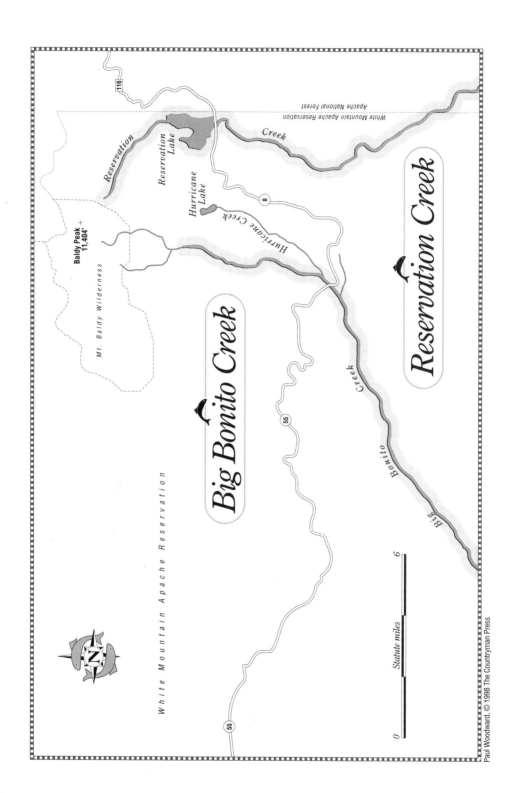

Big Bonito Creek

Reservation Creek

Baldy Peak
11,404'

Mt. Baldy Wilderness

White Mountain Apache Reservation

Apache National Forest
White Mountain Apache Reservation

Reservation

Reservation
Lake

Hurricane
Lake

Hurricane Creek

Creek

Creek

Bonito

Big

116

8

55

55

N

0   Statute miles   6

Route 73 crosses the North Fork and ends 3 miles upstream at the next road crossing.)

We returned to this same river four years later and found a different story. We fly-fished the same stretches without any success whatsoever—no strikes, no trout, not in more than two hours. What had happened to the North Fork in the Ditch Camp area in the intervening four years? We never did find out.

The North Fork of the White River begins near Mount Baldy at Sunrise Lake in the White Mountains and flows west, then southwest. You'll find planted trout as far downriver as the town of Fort Apache, where the East Fork of the White River joins. Several productive tributaries enter the North Fork and all have a good supply of trout.

In the Ditch Camp area the North Fork ranges from 20 to 30 feet wide and holds plenty of productive pools and riffles. Debris consisting of uprooted logs and brush has made many of these pools deeper and offers more protection for trout.

You can access the river at several points. You can reach the catch-and-release area on the upper end at Ditch Camp. Downriver several miles you can reach the river at Indian Route 473, as well as at the Williams Creek National Fish Hatchery on Indian Route 69. Ten miles downriver and 4.4 miles off of AZ 73 the Alchesay National Fish Hatchery, just upriver from the town of Whiteriver, provides access. From this hatchery you'll find a paved road paralleling the river for 5 miles. There's plenty of trout—*and* angling pressure—on the lower end of the North Fork from April through September. Authorities stock the stream often from April through September.

BEST TIMES TO FISH THE HATCHES

April 1–May 31
Little Black Stonefly: afternoon, size 16 or 18
Quill Gordon: afternoon, size 16
Blue Quill: morning, size 18
Little Blue-Winged Olive Dun: afternoon, size 20

June 1–August 31
Western Green Drake: morning, size 12 (upper area)
Tan Caddis: evening, size 14
Pale Evening Dun: evening, size 16
Green Caddis: size 14 or 16, evening
Trico: morning, size 24
Little Blue-Winged Olive Dun: afternoon, size 20

September 1–October 30
Trico: morning, size 24
Little Blue-Winged Olive Dun: afternoon, size 20

DIAMOND CREEK

Rating: 5
Access: Good
Seasons: Year-round
Maps: DeLorme p. 52, White Mountain Apache maps
Regulations: Tribal permit required
Positives: Easy access
Negatives: Extreme fishing pressure, small stream

Brian Williams works as a dentist Monday through Friday in the Mesa, Arizona, area. On weekends, though, you'll most often find him hunting or fly-fishing in the White Mountains. He's shot some trophy game in his lifetime. Diamond Creek near Whiteriver is a frequent fly-fishing destination on those trips to the White Mountains. Just this past year he caught a 19-inch rainbow on this small, heavily fished stream.

Diamond Creek begins just south of the origin of the North Fork of the White River, and just north of the East Fork. There's about 10 miles

RON DUNGAN

RON DUNGAN

Hawley Lake, near Trout Creek

of small-stream fishing on Diamond. At its mouth the stream ranges from 10 to 15 feet wide and holds many small pools and pockets. Throughout the 10 miles you'll find rocks and some larger boulders strewn across the stream. The (sort of) improved dirt Indian Route 61 parallels much of the lower end, and herein lies one of the major problems with Diamond Creek—fishing pressure. As you travel upstream on Indian Route 61 you'll see plenty of evidence of this pressure. Still, Diamond Creek does receive plantings of Apache trout, so you should also find plenty of trout from May through August.

Hatches? You'll find a few, but don't expect to see a major hatch or many trout surface feeding. Diamond Creek does hold some caddisflies throughout the season. I found that a Beadhead Pheasant Tail Nymph in size 16 works well here.

Diamond Creek enters the North Fork of the White River a few miles north of the town of Whiteriver.

BEST TIMES TO FISH THE HATCHES

April 1–May 31
Little Blue-Winged Olive Dun: afternoon, size 20
Little Brown Stonefly: afternoon, size 16 or 18

June 1–August 31
Tan Caddis: evening, size 14 or 16
Little Yellow Stonefly: evening, size 16
Pale Evening Dun: evening, size 16
Trico: morning, size 24

September 1–October 31
Little Blue-Winged Olive Dun: afternoon, size 20

TROUT CREEK

Rating: 6
Access: Difficult to Fair
Seasons: Sp, S, F
Maps: DeLorme p. 52, White Mountain Apache maps
Regulations: Tribal permit needed
Positives: Plenty of stream to fish, little angling pressure in the middle section
Negatives: Difficult to fish at some spots, some angling pressure just below the lake

Don't head for Trout Creek too early in the season. I thought late April would be an excellent time to fish this productive stream a couple of years ago—but it wasn't. Virgil Bradford and I turned right off AZ 260 a few miles west of Pinetop-Lakeside onto Indian Route 473 and traveled 9 miles to Hawley Lake. Three-foot snowdrifts along the highway should have alerted us to the condition of our destination, Trout Creek. When we arrived at the spillway, we hiked down a trail to the stream below. In its first couple of hundred feet Trout Creek holds a few beaver ponds, some pocket water, and very difficult fly-fishing. Small willows growing along the shore seem to grab each fly cast in their direction. And on this particular day, the water was still too cold.

If you have a day to explore and you don't want to see other anglers, spend some time on this productive stream. Just below Hawley Lake it averages 20 to 30 feet wide with plenty of small islands. Below this it ranges from 15 to 25 feet wide.

You'll see insects on the water. Trout Creek holds some blue quills and the ever-present little blue-winged olive dun.

There's some angling pressure in the beaver ponds just below the dam. Walk downstream a mile or two to get away from the crowds.

Trout Creek flows southeasterly for about 10 miles until it empties into the North Fork of the White River. You can access the stream from the top at Hawley Lake, or from the bottom via Indian Route 65. Access the middle section on Indian Route 652, which closely parallels the stream.

BEST TIMES TO FISH THE HATCHES

May 1–June 30
Little Brown Stonefly: afternoon, size 16 or 18
Little Blue-Winged Olive Dun: afternoon, size 20
Blue Quill: morning, size 18
Green Caddis: evening, size 14
Western Green Drake: morning, size 12

July 1–September 30
Tan Caddis: evening, size 14 or 16
Pale Evening Dun: evening, size 16
Little Blue-Winged Olive Dun: afternoon, size 20
Green Caddis: evening, size 14
Trico: morning, size 24 (spotty)

PARADISE CREEK

Rating: 5
Access: Fair
Seasons: Sp, S, F
Maps: DeLorme p. 52, White Mountain Apache maps
Regulations: Tribal permit required
Positives: Not much pressure
Negatives: Small stream, tough casting

Are you tired of the crowds on the North Fork of the White River? Then try one of the White Mountain Apache tribe's smaller, productive, stocked streams, one that's just a short distance downriver from the North Fork at Ditch Camp. Travel on AZ 260 east of Pinetop-Lakeside to Indian Route 473. Cross the North Fork of the White River at McCoy Bridge, and bear left onto Indian Route 59. This will take you to Paradise Creek, a small stream that holds some decent trout and good hatches. The stream's open for 3 miles—you'll see posters showing you where it's closed.

This stream is not for the faint of heart. It's a difficult place to fly-cast—only 15 to 20 feet wide. Little blue-winged olives appear here in late May and early April; the same hatch appears again in September and October.

Paradise is definitely a late-spring, summer, and early-fall stream. Much of winter the road to Hawley Lake is open but Indian Route 59, accessing Paradise Creek, is usually closed. The elevation at the stream is about 8000 feet. If you enjoy challenging, small-stream situations this might be worth a try.

BEST TIMES TO FISH THE HATCHES

April 1–May 31
Little Blue-Winged Olive Dun: afternoon, size 24
Little Brown Stonefly: afternoon, size 16 or 18
Blue Quill: morning, size 18

June 1–August 31
Green Caddis: evening, size 14
Tan Caddis: evening, size 14 or 16
Western Green Drake: morning, size 12
Little Blue-Winged Olive Dun: afternoon, size 20
Pale Evening Dun: evening, size 16
Trico: morning, size 24 (spotty)
Dark Brown Dun: morning and afternoon, size 14

September 1–October 31
Little Blue-Winged Olive Dun: afternoon, size 20
Trico: morning, size 24

EAST FORK OF THE WHITE RIVER

Rating: 6
Access: Good
Seasons: Year-round
Maps: DeLorme p. 52, White Mountain Apache maps
Regulations: Tribal permit required; the section upriver from Indian Route 60 is closed
Positives: A classic western stream, plenty of fast water with deep pockets and pools, good cool water, easy to reach, some large brown trout
Negatives: Angling pressure

What a day of fishing! We had traveled on dirt roads for more than 100 miles, fished several small streams for Apache trout, saw two large herds of elk, watched some wild turkeys feed in a cienega, and saw a herd of wild horses. How could we ever close this particular day without a letdown?

For a finale we fished for a couple of hours on the East Fork of the White River. Even at this time in late May it was running high from snowmelt from Baldy Peak. Josh David of Pine Top, Craig Josephson, and I fanned out along the stream and picked out productive-looking pools or riffles to begin. Indian Route 55 closely parallels the lower end of the East Fork and you're only a few feet from good fishing.

I used a heavily weighted Woolly Bugger to get deep in the high water. It must have been on my second or third cast that for several seconds my Bugger stayed motionless. I felt sure I had hung up on the bottom—then with a quick surge the fly moved upriver. Soon I felt the tug of a heavy trout irritated by that Bugger in its mouth. For more than 10 minutes that trout moved upstream, then downstream, then under a huge boulder at my feet, where it became entangled in several rocks. Finally the trout broke off—but before it did I had a chance to view it, all 20-plus inches of brown trout. Yes, the East Fork holds some heavy fish!

You'll find plenty of rocks and boulders lining the East Fork. Fish all the pools and pockets formed by these barriers. The East Fork begins near Baldy Peak, which is more than 11,000 feet high. As it flows west to join the North Fork of the White River it widens considerably. Upriver near Indian Route 60 you'll find a fast-flowing 20- to 30-foot-wide river. Down-

East Fork of the White River

river, just above Whiteriver, the stream widens to 40 to 50 feet. Remember, you can't fish upriver from Indian Route 60.

You'll see some hatches on the East Fork, like little blue wings, blue quills, and tricos on the lower end. This lower end, near the town of Fort Apache, also holds a decent trico hatch most summer mornings.

You can easily access the East Fork. Take Indian Route 46 east from Fort Apache. This road, then Indian Route 55, closely parallels the river to Rock Creek. East Fork above that point is closed to fishing.

BEST TIMES TO FISH THE HATCHES

March 1–May 15
Little Black Stonefly: afternoon, size 16
Little Blue-Winged Olive Dun: afternoon, size 20
Blue Quill: morning, size 18
Quill Gordon: afternoon, size 16

May 15–August 31
Pale Evening Dun: evening, size 16
Trico: morning, size 24 (lower end)
Tan Caddis: evening, size 16
Dark Brown Dun: morning and afternoon, size 14

September 1–October 31
Little Blue-Winged Olive Dun: afternoon, size 20
Trico: morning, size 24

LOFER CIENEGA CREEK

Rating: 6
Access: Fair
Seasons: Sp, S, F
Maps: DeLorme p. 53; White Mountain Apache maps
Regulations: Catch-and-release only; tribal permit required; closed upstream from Indian Route 55
Positives: spectacular scenery, an opportunity to catch streambred Apache trout, little angling pressure
Negatives: Dirt road for 30 miles, small stream

Not long ago Craig Josephson showed me an article in *Fly Rod & Reel* magazine about native trout fishing in the White Mountains of Arizona. The article suggested that a few high-altitude streams still held wild Apache trout. In all our years of fly-fishing we had never fished for this species.

Bob David was our guide for the day. Bob's done a lot to preserve this native species; he runs the hatchery for the Fort Apache Indian Reservation in Whiteriver. He suggested that we first try a spot on Indian Route 55. After 30 miles of dirt road and we finally arrived at our destination—Lofer Cienega Creek. Cienega is Spanish for "marsh, bog, or swamp." This stream would more properly be called Lofer Prado, or "meadow."

We worked our way downstream from the road for ½ mile through a heavy covering of pines and came to an opening in the forest. It was a huge meadow, 1 mile wide by 4 miles long. Suddenly the root-infested, log-choked, difficult-to-fish stream became wide open, with few obstacles to casting to the trout. As I glanced around I saw three turkeys run toward some nearby brush; beyond them a herd of wild horses looked at us, and then ran for the cover of the pine forest.

Craig, Josh David, (Bob David's son), and I took turns fishing the pools on this 10- to 15-foot-wide alpine stream. In almost every pool we caught Apache trout. Few reached 7 inches in length, but we caught plenty of them.

Don't miss this stream—and make certain you fish downstream to the *cienega* to experience this scenic wonder. Fishing is closed above Indian Route 55, but you can fish downstream a couple of miles until Lofer Cienega flows into Bonito Creek. If you have a day to spend and somebody to accompany you, you can fish downstream to Bonito Creek, then fish up Bonito to Indian Route 55. Here you can meet your fishing buddy.

I haven't encountered any great hatches on this small, productive stream, but you will see some blue quills, little blue-winged olives, and tricos.

Lofer Cienega flows just a few miles north of Big Bonito. You can reach it on Indian Routes 46 to 55 from Fort Apache. If you enjoy breathtaking scenery, wildlife, and catching small Apache trout, then you'll certainly like this one.

BEST TIMES TO FISH HATCHES

May 1–June 30
Little Blue-Winged Olive Dun: afternoon, size 20
Blue Quill: morning, size 18
Green Caddis: evening, size 16

July 1–September 30
Little Yellow Stonefly: evening, size 18
Blue Quill: morning, size 18
Little Blue-Winged Olive Dun: afternoon, size 20
Trico: morning, size 24 (very spotty)

BIG BONITO CREEK

Rating: 8
Access: Difficult
Seasons: Sp, S, F
Maps: DeLorme pp. 53, 60, 61; White Mountain Apache map
Regulations: Tribal permit required
Positives: Little fishing pressure, great population of wild trout, fantastic scenery
Negatives: Difficult to access

It was a day chock full of memorable events. Craig Josephson and I left Greer Lodge, located in the town of Greer, south of Springerville, and headed onto 100 miles of dirt roads—most either forest or Indian improved dirt roads—looking to fish and to explore. First we headed south on Forest Road (FR) 87 to FR 113 and fished the upper end of the West Fork of the Little Colorado. We continued on FR 113 and then took FR 116 to Reservation Lake to fish the stream to the south, looking for some large rainbows. Almost as soon as we arrived in this magnificent open alpine meadow, a huge thunderhead overhead spewed lightning bolts across the valley. I'm scared of lightning. As a 10-year-old kid I saw my neighbor hit by a bolt. When lightning occurs now I scurry for the safety of a car or home. But this time neither of these two safeguards was close by, so we ran the 2 miles to our car and headed out of the area.

By the way, you should be scared of lightning, too. Just the day before this adventure, lightning struck an angler fishing Reservation Lake. When you encounter lightning storms in this high country, save fishing for another time.

We then took Indian Route 8 and turned right onto Indian Route 55, another Apache dirt road, and made our way to our next destination, Big Bonito Creek. After what seemed like several hours we arrived. (The easier way in is from Whiteriver, as explained later.) I was tired and didn't expect too much from this stream, so I stayed in the car while Craig fished the spillway just below the culvert. Soon I heard a loud shrill. When I got out of the car to see what had happened, Craig was hoisting a heavy streambred brown trout from the stream below. Suddenly I wasn't so tired. I gathered my gear from the trunk and headed for the creek. Craig and I hiked downstream ½ mile until we hit some high walls and huge boulders. We would try the section below another day.

Big Bonito in this area ranges from 15 to 20 feet wide and contains deep boulder-strewn pools and plenty of pocket water. The water has a dark brown color, and I measured it at 54 degrees on that May day.

Craig worked a deep pool below me with a huge boulder in the middle and a sheer cliff on its far side. Before I could even make my first cast Craig caught his second streambred brown on a Beadhead Hare's Ear. I cast to an eddy near the far shore and a trout swirled at my dry fly. On the second cast the fish hit, and I landed a dark brown trout that matched the color of the water. While Craig remained in the deep pool below I worked my way upstream, fishing each pocket as I walked along the bank. Almost each productive-looking place held a brown trout—some more than one.

Craig finally left his huge pool and worked his way upstream. I watched as he cast a Beadhead into a short, deep run. On the first cast a 15-inch brown hit that pattern. He landed the trout and we both headed upstream toward the car. What a fantastic one-hour fishing event that turned out to be!

Big Bonito holds some great hatches, along with terrestrials throughout the season. The day Craig and I fished here in late May we saw a tremendous number of winged ants on the surface; trout were feeding freely on them. At the right time of the season you'll also find some pale morning duns and blue quills emerging throughout much of Big Bonito Creek.

You can reach the stream from Whiteriver by way of the East Fork of the White River: Take 73 south to Fort Apache, then follow 46 east along the East Fork to Indian Route 55. Turn right, away from the East Fork, on 55. You'll travel about 15 miles on this dirt road before you hit Big Bonito Creek.

The route into Big Bonito can be rough and rutted. Don't travel this road if you expect rain. Still, it's a trip that can be as exhilarating as the fishing on the stream: I've seen hundreds of elk cross this road. It's well worth the price of the permit.

Big Bonito has plenty of deep pools formed by ledges, boulders, and smaller rocks. Each pool and riffle upstream seems to hold trout, especially brown trout. After you hike downstream a mile or so you can be certain few other anglers have fished this water. Don't forget that above Indian Route 55 Big Bonito is closed to fishing.

Big Bonito ranks up there with the Black River, the Little Colorado, and the Colorado at Lee's Ferry as one of the top streams in the state. Treat this stream with respect and return each and every trout you catch here. And don't forget, you are a guest on this Fort Apache Indian Reservation, and you've been given the opportunity to fish one of Arizona's gems.

BEST TIMES TO FISH THE HATCHES

April 1–May 31
Little Blue-Winged Olive Dun: afternoon, size 20
Little Brown Stonefly: afternoon, size 16

Blue Quill: morning, size 18
Quill Gordon: afternoon, size 14
Black Ant: all day, size 14 to 16
Pale Morning Dun: evening, size 16

June 1–August 31
Dark Brown Dun: afternoon, size 14
Western Green Drake: morning, size 12
Pale Evening Dun: evening: size 16
Tan Caddis: evening, size 14 or 16
Little Yellow Stonefly: evening, size 16
Trico: morning, size 24

September 1–October 30
Trico: morning, size 24
Little Blue-Winged Olive Dun: afternoon, size 20

RESERVATION CREEK

Rating: 5
Access: Difficult to Fair
Seasons: Sp, S, F
Maps: DeLorme p. 53, White Mountain Apache map
Regulations: Tribal permit required
Positives: Spectacular scenery, little angling pressure
Negatives: Difficult to reach, few trout during summer

Were the reports we had heard about large trout on Reservation Creek true? Several anglers and guides at Greer Lodge had told us about some huge rainbows that move up this creek early in spring. Were we too late to hit this migration?

Craig Josephson and I traveled from Greer Lodge north on 373 for 2 miles, then turned left on dirt Forest Road (FR) 87, Badger Creek Road. We took another left on FR 113, crossed the Little Colorado River, then traveled 15 miles to Reservation Lake on Indian Route 8. (Maps will also list FR 116 in this area; be aware that the roads can be confusing.) We parked here at the lake, hiked down a steep bank below the dam, and headed toward the stream. The first ½ mile of Reservation Creek below the dam flows through a thick pine forest, dropping considerably. Then the stream enters a *cienega* and slows to a meander. In this open meadow Reservation looks a lot like Lofer Cienega Creek, 15 air miles to the southeast. We fished each pool expecting to catch one of the lunker trout that we had heard about—but we didn't even catch a small one. Craig and I surmised that the water here must warm considerably, and that trout must move in late April to spawn and then leave before the stream temperatures rise above 70 degrees.

We hiked down the meandering stream and decided to fish the 1-mile stretch where the stream flowed through the open meadow. Then I looked skyward, saw a huge dark cloud coming toward us, and alerted Craig. Within an hour a horrendous thunderstorm appeared and we ran the full mile back to the safety of our car. We never learned if Reservation Creek really does hold trout, or if those fish use it for anything more. If you plan to fish this stream try doing it in late April or very early May—that is, if you can get to the water that early in the season.

At the very lower end of the stream, before it enters the Black River off the reservation, the creek does hold a good number of trout. You can reach this stretch by taking FR 25 to the east off US 191. Travel that gravel road for about 20 miles.

And always look out for those severe thunderstorms that can appear here.

BEST TIMES TO FISH THE HATCHES

April 1–May 31
Little Blue-Winged Olive Dun: afternoon, size 20
Blue Quill: morning, size 18
Quill Gordon: afternoon, size 16

June 1–September 30
Little Blue-Winged Olive Dun: afternoon, size 20
Blue Quill: morning, size 18
Pale Evening Dun: evening, size 16
Little Yellow Stonefly: evening, size 16
Trico: morning, size 24 (very spotty)

7

High Country—Northeastern Arizona and Far Western New Mexico

The high country, including Show Low, Pinetop-Lakeside, Springerville, Eagar, and Alpine in Arizona, and Reserve in New Mexico, is a spectacular area, and it boasts plenty of potentially good trout streams. But the future of trout fishing in this far eastern part of Arizona, especially stream fishing, looks bleak. Many of the streams once stocked with trout—Eagle Creek and the Blue River, for example—no longer receive fish. Why? Local anglers blame it on growing concern for returning or saving native fish in some of the streams. The counter argument to this is that when the streams were stocked, it had no effect on the numbers of native fish. Dozens of anglers and residents voiced the same thought to me over and over again— stock the streams with trout and stop worrying about the native fish. In the meantime, while Arizona Game and Fish looks out for native fish, the trout streams in the area will suffer. Many anglers have shifted to lake fishing because so few streams receive planted trout.

But despite the drawbacks, Arizona's high country has some great streams, too. Several years ago Craig Josephson of Syracuse, New York, and I fished this area in late May. We headed southeast from Greer toward the Little Colorado River. Several miles from Greer we encountered some deep snowbanks—remember, this was late May. We fished the Little Colorado and Black Rivers for the next three days, never once at an altitude below 9000 feet. Even in midsummer you'll find comfortable temperatures here. And you'll see plenty of snow. Hannagan Meadows, at over 9000 feet, just south of Alpine, often holds snow in sheltered areas well into May.

West Fork of the Black River

Travel east from Alpine about 30 miles and you're in New Mexico trout country. Here you'll see streams like the San Francisco River, Willow Creek, and the South Fork of Negrito Creek. Isolated in far western New Mexico, these and a couple of other trout streams merit your attention. Some of the best fly-fishing I've experienced in the past few years has occurred on New Mexico waters.

The rivers and streams of the high country hold plenty of trout and some great hatches. Both the Little Colorado and Black Rivers hold good trico hatches from July through much of September. You'll also find plenty of waters that host green drakes, pale morning duns, little blue-winged olives, and blue quills. Downwings are plentiful too; brown and green caddis usually appear in June and July, and the little yellow stonefly in early July.

If you enjoy stillwater fly-fishing then the high country has plenty to offer you. Within 50 miles lie top trout waters like Big Lake, Nelson Reservoir, Luna Lake, and Hulsey Lake. Nelson Reservoir boasts the Arizona state-record rainbow trout, and Luna Lake the trophy cutthroat.

Don't overlook some of the smaller tributaries of the Black, Little Colorado, and Gila Rivers. Many of these hold trout and get little angling pressure.

This area is worth a visit for other reasons, too. You've got to stay for a day or two in the town of Springerville. In all my trips across the United

States I have not found a friendlier spot on the map. Stop by the Sports Shack, the oldest sporting goods store in the White Mountains. It carries over 10,000 flies that range from 69 to 99 cents—a deal found nowhere else in Arizona

About 30 miles south of Springerville you'll find the quaint town of Alpine. Where did Alpine get its name? You guessed it—at 8000 feet, this town looks out of place in Arizona. If you want to get away from the heat of the desert, Alpine is the place to do it.

And just once in your lifetime, travel south on the Coronado Highway (US 191) from Alpine to Clifton. This may be the most breathtaking trip I've ever taken. Don't expect to make time on this road, however. The term *hairpin curve* must have originated on this scenic, magnificent, sometimes dangerous highway.

BLACK RIVER

Rating: 8
Access: Fair to Poor
Seasons: Sp, S, F
Maps: DeLorme pp. 53, 61; White Mountain Apache maps
Regulations: Tribal permit required
Positives: The best river in the state for wild trout, tremendous scenery, uncrowded, plenty of wildlife
Negatives: Poor access to many stretches, tough walking

I had heard a muffled bawling behind me and turned just in time to see a yearling black bear cub take a plunge into the river. Two quick strides and he was across and up the far bank in the blink of an eye. I was thinking how lucky I was to see such a sight—until I realized that my fishing buddy, Monty Peters, and I had separated the cub from his mother. The next few minutes were a little tense, but we never glimpsed her. We considered ourselves fortunate indeed and went about our primary goal, to catch some of the Black River's trout.

Sights like this are not uncommon while fishing the remote waters of the Black River in east-central Arizona. Bears are common in this rugged area, as are turkey, elk, deer, and other wild animals. It always adds to a trip when you can see some of the wildlife of the region.

But please be careful. I have been to the Black many times and never had trouble with bears, but I've also seen some camps here trashed by one that had a nose for the goodies left around. Be sure to put all your food in your vehicle while you head upstream; better yet, hang it in a tree, from a branch that a bear can't get to. Problem bears are removed from the area every year, so it's better to be safe than sorry.

The Black serves as the border between the White Mountain Apache and San Carlos Apache Reservations in eastern Arizona. Truly the gem of both tribes, the Black's headwaters begin high in eastern Arizona. The West Fork comes off Mount Baldy, the East Fork comes from around Big Lake, and the North Fork starts as series of springs in the Apache National Forest. All three forks join at an elevation of around 6500 feet and flow westerly, dropping to 4500 feet. Forty-five miles downstream, the Black joins the White to form the Salt, the main water source for the fast-growing metropolitan Phoenix area. (I always thought the Salt should have been named the Gray, but I guess that would have been too logical—and not very stylish.)

The upper East Fork of the Black is my favorite section. It's predominantly trout water. Late in summer, after the waters have warmed, larger smallmouth will get up into some of the upper reaches, but I've never caught any earlier in the spring. Browns, rainbows, and native Apaches are the dominant species from roughly Ten of Diamonds upriver to the San Carlos Indian Reservation border. The Ten of Diamonds area is the uppermost access to the river's edge. Indian Route 2034 crisscrosses the river six times with ample, although simple, camping areas in designated sites. Although there are no toilet facilities, there are some picnic tables provided, and fire rings from previous campers. Use common sense if you plan to ford the river in your vehicle. Cross only when the flow permits it. I guarantee that paying the towing bill to be pulled from the Black will make you regret trying to cross during high water. Crossing by foot can be even more dangerous.

The condition of the river depends totally on the snowpack from the previous winter. It's usually fishable by mid-May, but I've also seen it blown out at that time, so check with the local fly shops if you're planning an early-spring trip; you may save yourself a long ride on a muddy road. The roads into and out of the Black can also be a four-wheeler's nightmare if you try them too soon. It's always best to go in with at least two vehicles (and towropes) when possible.

As the waters warm in summer the smallmouth fishing gets good. Drifting a Woolly Bugger or dark stonefly with plenty of weight to get it down will usually work well for the feisty bass. Most are 8 to 10 inches, but I've taken many up to 3 pounds—and even an 8-incher in this small stream is a great fight on a 3-weight! A Girdle Bug is also a good pattern, and lately I've been tying a small Sparkle Bugger with rubber legs and bead-chain eyes. The eyes turn the hook upside down, making it less likely to

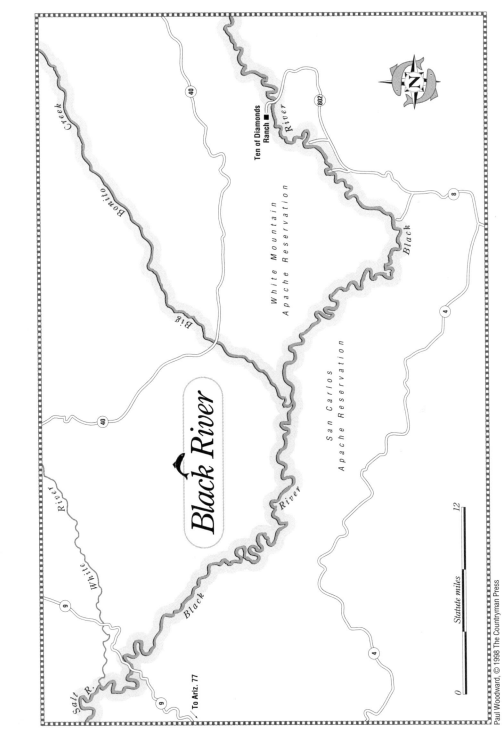

Black River

Bonito Creek

40

Ten of Diamonds
Ranch ■

River

802

8

White Mountain
Apache Reservation

Black

Big

4

San Carlos
Apache Reservation

River

Black

River

40

White

River

9

Black

River

4

Salt R.

9

To Ariz. 77

0   12

Statute miles

Paul Woodward. © 1998 The Countryman Press

become a permanent fixture on the rocky bottom. You'll pick up your share of trout with this method as well. The Apaches and browns seem to like it more than the rainbows, which prefer the usual Hare's Ears and Pheasant Tails (beadheads in particular), and readily take dry flies. During warmer weather there are abundant caddis hatches, little yellow stoneflies, and many kinds of mayflies. The hatch chart that follows lists some of the more common hatches.

Terrestrials work well in mid- and late summer. Hoppers are a good bet. I remember catching my first native Apache with a hopper. He was working at the head of a riffle and, when he took, screamed downstream with me in hot pursuit. After a lengthy battle, I was cradling a chunky 18-inch trout without a clue as to what it was. It looked like a rainbow without the stripe, but had yellow fins. Not until a few years later did I realize I had caught one of Arizona's very own wild trout.

By the way, I should mention that the protected bonytail chub, indigenous to the Black, will readily take a dry fly. If you happen to catch any of these fish, handle them carefully and release them unharmed. They are school fish and are prolific in certain areas of the river, usually the pools.

The river has an abundance of crawdads and hellgrammites, and trout dine on them whenever they get the chance. The key is to get your fly down to the bottom. Use a heavy tippet—at least 3X—or you may as well just throw all your flies in the river and get it over with, because that's where they'll end up. When the water clears later in the season you may have to go lighter, but I usually stick with 3X fluorocarbon, making sure that when I change my tippet, I put the old one in my pocket. The Black is a "pack it in, pack it out" area; please respect that.

Access is from both the White Mountain and the San Carlos sides of the river. Below Ten of Diamonds are several points where you can get your vehicle to the water's edge, and a few that end high on the canyon rim above the river. The latter do feature trails leading down to the river. Although there are well-kept paths, they are steep and will test city legs and lungs. I like to camp on the river's edge for just that reason—after a long day of hiking the river, I am not looking forward to a steep hike straight up to camp.

The Black River is a special use area and requires a permit for camping and fishing. A Black River permit will cost you $10 a day; it entitles you to camp and fish for one day, and it expires at midnight, so don't be caught here after that time. You can spend the night if you have a permit for the next day. Permits can be bought from both of the tribes, so be sure to camp on the same side of the river that you purchased the permit.

BEST TIMES TO FISH THE HATCHES

April 1–June 15
Little Brown Stonefly: afternoon, size 16 or 18
Little Blue-Winged Olive Dun: afternoon, size 20
Quill Gordon: afternoon, size 16
Grannom: size 16, afternoon and evening
Pale Morning Dun: morning and evening, size 16
Blue Quill: morning, size 18
Pale Evening Dun: evening, size 16
Little Black Stonefly: evening, size 16

June 15–August 31
Little Yellow Stonefly: evening, size 16
Trico: morning, size 24
Green Caddis: evening, size 16
Tan Caddis: evening, size 14

September 1–October 31
Little Blue-Winged Olive Dun: afternoon, size 20
Trico: morning: size 24
Blue Quill: morning; size 18

EAST FORK OF THE BLACK RIVER

BEST TIMES TO FISH THE HATCHES

April 1–May 31
Little Blue-Winged Olive Dun: afternoon, size 20
Little Brown Stonefly: afternoon, sizes 16 and 18
Pale Morning Dun: morning, size 16
Grannom: afternoon, size 16

June 1–September 30
Pale Morning Dun: morning, size 16
Trico: morning, size 24

WEST FORK OF THE BLACK RIVER

April 1–May 31
Little Blue-Winged Olive Dun: afternoon, size 20
Blue Quill: morning, size 18

Pale Morning Dun: morning, size 16
Quill Gordon: afternoon, size 14
Little Brown Stonefly: afternoon, size 16
Grannom: afternoon, size 16

June 1–September 30
Tan Caddis: evening, size 14 or 16
Pale Morning Dun: morning, size 16
Pale Evening Dun: evening, size 16
Trico: morning, size 24

LITTLE COLORADO RIVER, EAST AND WEST FORKS

Rating: 7
Access: Good
Seasons: Year-round
Maps: DeLorme p. 53, White Mountain Apache maps
Positives: Private stretches hold plenty of trout and are relatively inexpensive to fish; plenty of streambred and native trout; good cold water in upper 15 miles; some good hatches
Negatives: Some private stretches, warms up near Eagar, small stream, heavily fished on West Fork

Many years ago, Craig Josephson set up an entire week of fly-fishing and invited me to join him—in Arizona. A week of fly-fishing in Arizona? I seriously doubted that Arizona had any quality fly-fishing waters. But it turned out to be one of the most unusual fly-fishing trips I've ever taken. And what a way to end it—with a full day at the X-Diamond Ranch on the Little Colorado River, near Eagar. That last day I changed my mind about Arizona completely. For six hours Craig and I landed one trout after another—many over 15 inches long. A few browns hit the assortment of flies we presented, but it was the heavy rainbows that showed us the quality of fishing that the river held. We ended the day—and the trip—exhausted but jubilant.

Four years later Virgil Bradford of Santa Fe, New Mexico, and I returned to the X-Diamond Ranch for another day of fly-fishing. Virgil began fly-fishing just four years ago, but his prowess far belies his number of years of experience. He's an excellent nymph-fisher and usually uses a tandem of a Woolly Bugger and a Beadhead Pheasant Tail Nymph.

We arrived at the ranch two days after the official beginning of spring.

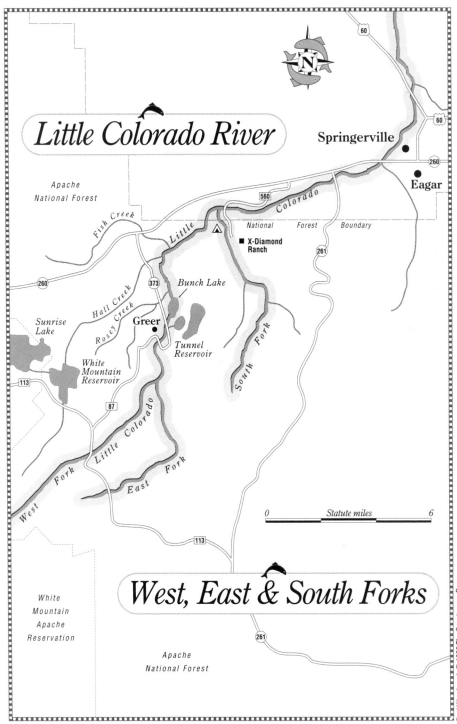

Little Colorado River

West, East & South Forks

Paul Woodward, © 1998 The Countryman Press

A favorite section of the Little Colorado River near the X-Diamond Ranch

Driving in, we sure didn't believe that spring had arrived. As we passed Mount Baldy we saw fields still covered with 3-foot snowdrifts. We'd left Phoenix the day before with temperatures in the low 90s; here they struggled to rise into the 60s. At the ranch itself, just 20 miles from Mount Baldy, much of the snow had melted. But the snowmelt from higher elevations made the river run high and a bit off-color.

When I recorded a 45-degree water temperature I feared we would have a barren day. Not so! Virgil and I experienced one of the best days of fly-fishing that either of us had seen anywhere in recent years. We estimated that we landed 35 trout, lost another 20, and had maybe 20 more strikes. Fifteen of the trout we landed were over 15 inches long; four measured over 18 inches. What a day! What a river! What a place to fly-fish.

The X-Diamond has a modest fee schedule; you can enjoy a full day of fly-fishing for less than the cost a pair of hipboots, $35. You can also choose a half day's fishing. Winkie Crigler, owner of the ranch, will make you feel at home. Wink also offers great accommodations. She rents five cabins on the ranch, most with spectacular views of the valley. And by the way, you've got to sample one of Wink's famous chocolate chip cookies when you're here. For more information on this great river and for directions to the X-Diamond Ranch, call (520) 333-2286.

The Little Colorado River begins near one of Arizona's highest peaks,

Mount Baldy; it flows east, then north, to empty into the Colorado River near the Grand Canyon. You'll find trout in all three branches of the river—the East, West, and South Forks—as well as in tributaries like Hall, Rosey, and Fish Creeks. As the West Fork flows past the Greer Lodge in the alpine village of Greer you'll see a small, cold mountain stream that averages 10 to 15 feet wide. Just a couple of hundred feet below the lodge the West and East Forks join. You can reach the upper end of the East Fork on Forest Road (FR) 113. For the first 15 miles the river makes its way through some national forest land. Below that you'll find private land, but still plenty of trout.

Just above Greer is a 2-mile stretch reachable only by hiking. Here you'll find plenty of wild trout. Above this section you can reach the West Fork at Sheeps Crossing near Lee's Valley. The state plants plenty of trout in this section, but you'll also find plenty of angling pressure. When Craig Josephson and I checked the water temperature on this section of the river in late May we recorded a reading of 40 degrees. In the Sheeps Crossing area you'll find a mountain stream about 10 feet wide and difficult to fly-fish. Each willow and pine growing along bank the seems to grab your fly every time you cast.

The X-Diamond Ranch is about 20 miles downriver from the source. Just below the ranch the South Fork enters. The South Fork is a small stream—less than 10 feet wide—with some native trout. I consider the Little Colorado a small stream, and to fish it properly you should use small-stream tactics. It has plenty of small pools and productive riffles. The X-Diamond Ranch has plenty of beaver ponds where some large trout hold.

You can even see some green drakes on the South Fork in late May and early June. After the South Fork enters, the Little Colorado ranges from 15 to 25 feet wide. The state stocks trout in the Little Colorado River just below the X-Diamond Ranch. Bob Tulk of nearby Alpine often fishes the Little Colorado from the confluence of the South Fork downriver to Springerville. He does well in this lower area. Remember to respect private property here.

If you plan to stay at the Greer Lodge you'll have an added bonus: a couple of ponds next to the West Fork of the Little Colorado River are loaded with heavy rainbow trout. It's worth a stay at the lodge—which also conducts fly-fishing lessons with two fantastic instructors, Bob Pollock and Dana Bagnoli. Both conduct individual and group sessions and know the area streams well. Manager Gerald Scott is a fine host; he and X-Diamond Ranch owner Winkie Crigler can tell you the condition of the river.

BEST TIMES TO FISH THE HATCHES

March 1–April 30
Little Blue-Winged Olive Dun: afternoon, size 24
Little Brown Stonefly: afternoon, size 16 or 18

May 1–June 30
Little Yellow Stonefly: evening, size 16
Black Quill: afternoon, size 14
Little Blue-Winged Olive Dun: afternoon; size 20
Blue Quill: morning, size 18
Pale Evening Dun: evening, size 16
Pale Morning Dun: morning and evening, sizes 16 and 18
Western Green Drake: morning, size 12 (East, West, and South Fork)
Trico: morning, size 24
Brown Caddis: evening, size 14
Green Caddis: evening, size 14
Golden Stonefly: afternoon, size 14

July 1–August 31
Trico: morning, size 24
Flying Cinnamon Ant: all day, size 14

September 1–November 30
Little Blue-Winged Olive Dun: afternoon, size 20
Trico: morning, size 24

WEST FORK OF THE LITTLE COLORADO

BEST TIMES TO FISH THE HATCHES

April 15–May 31
Little Blue-Winged Olive Dun: afternoon, size 20
Quill Gordon: afternoon, size 14
Little Brown Stonefly: afternoon, size 16 or 18

June 1–September 30
Western Green Drake: morning, size 12
Tan Caddis: evening, size 14 or 16
Little Yellow Stonefly: evening, size 16

EAST FORK OF THE LITTLE COLORADO

BEST TIMES TO FISH THE HATCHES

April 15–May 31
Little Brown Stonefly: afternoon, size 16 or 18
Little Blue-Winged Olive Dun: afternoon, size 20
Blue Quill: morning, size 18

June 1–September 30
Western Green Drake: morning, size 12
Tan Caddis: evening, size 14 or 16
Trico: morning, size 24 (spotty)

LITTLE COLORADO RIVER, SOUTH FORK

Rating: 5
Access: Fair
Seasons: Sp, S, F
Maps: DeLorme p. 53, White Mountain Apache maps
Positives: Stream improvement devices in place in the campground, some good hatches for a small stream, little angling pressure once you hike upriver a mile or two
Negatives: Small, brushy stream; gets low in summer

I crossed over this stream dozens of times on my way to the X-Diamond Ranch, and it always looked small and uninteresting. Then, just recently, I found out that the South Fork of the Little Colorado River holds some of the great western hatches, like the pale morning dun, the blue quill, and the western green drake.

It's extremely small and runs low in the summer, but the South Fork holds brown and rainbow trout. If you park at the campground and hike upriver you'll find them. Upriver from the campground about 2 miles you'll also see a few old beaver ponds, which hold plenty of trout. Just like any stream-living brown trout, those on the South Fork get extremely spooky, especially in low water conditions.

The South Fork looks like a typical productive trout stream—plenty of small pools and riffles—but don't expect to see many large pools. It hosts the classic western hatches and even a few tricos. Look for the drake to appear in early to mid-June. You'll note some stream improvements in the campground area. It averages 10 to 15 feet wide. Arizona Game and

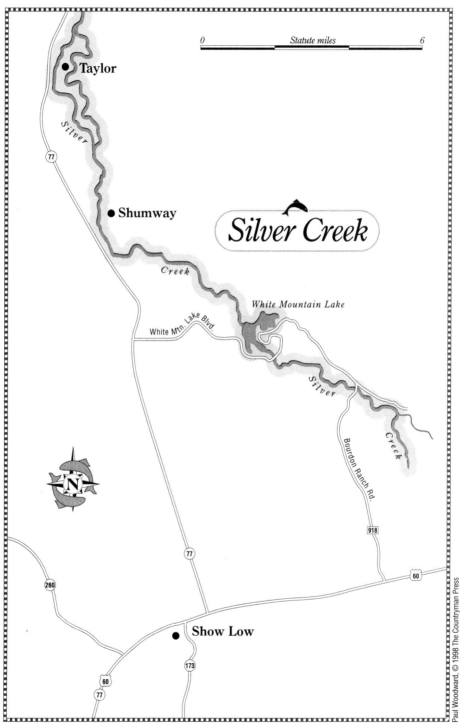

Taylor

Silver

77

Shumway

Creek

Silver Creek

0   Statute miles   6

White Mountain Lake

White Mtn. Lake Blvd

Silver

Creek

Bourdon Ranch Rd.

918

N

77

60

260

Show Low

173

60

77

Fish unloads trout just a mile downstream. (They could very easily plant some trout in the campground area.)

You can reach the river from AZ 260. If you're traveling east from Springerville, turn right onto South Fork Road (FR 560) and continue 3 miles to the campground.

BEST TIMES TO FISH THE HATCHES

April 1–May 31
Little Blue-Winged Olive Dun: afternoon, size 20
Quill Gordon: afternoon, size 16
Blue Quill: morning, size 18

June 1–September 30
Western Green Drake: morning, size 12
Pale Evening Dun: evening, size 16
Trico: morning, size 24
Tan Caddis: evening, size 14 or 16
Little Blue-Winged Olive Dun: afternoon, size 20

SILVER CREEK

Rating: 5
Access: Good
Seasons: Sp, S, F
Maps: DeLorme p. 52, Sitgreaves National Forest maps
Positives: Easy access, good early-season hatches, little pressure, easy casting, short walking distance to the stream, clear during runoff on other local streams
Negatives: small stream, poorly marked

Don't tell me trout don't rise a few minutes after they're stocked. They did on Silver Creek.

For the entire morning of April 16 Virgil Bradford and I fished under brilliant blue skies—then clouds—then heavy snow squalls. Between it all we managed to keep our lines on the water for an hour or so. Then about 1:30 PM an Arizona Game and Fish stocking truck drove in and dumped several buckets of healthy rainbow trout right in front of us.

Within 10 minutes of their arrival these trout began feeding on the surface. Just ask Arizona Game and Fish employee Ken McGown—with me and Virgil, he watched in amazement as the newly planted trout rose to a hatch of little blue-winged olives. Overcast skies and cool temperatures

A trout recently stocked on Silver Creek

prevented the thousands of emerging insects from taking flight, and the newly planted trout feasted.

So Virgil tied on a size 20 Little Blue-Winged Olive—yes, a size 20 dry fly—and caught a trout on his first cast. The action continued until 3 PM when another snow squall appeared and we headed for the car. We hadn't done badly—30 trout caught and released. Many of these were caught on dry flies. And don't forget that these trout were freshly stocked. Talk about bad days turning good—that day on Silver Creek certainly did!

The following day Brian Williams of Gilbert joined us. I handed him a size 20 Little Blue-Winged Olive Dun and asked him to cast it toward a pod of more than a dozen rising trout. In 10 casts Brian had 10 strikes. (You'll see this pattern listed in chapter 10; the olive Super Micro Vernille tied in as an extended body creates one of the finest patterns I've ever used.)

You can reach Silver Creek on US 60. About 7 miles north of Show Low, take Bourdon Ranch Road. Go about 5 miles until you see Hatchery Way on your right. Take this rutted dirt road to the creek. To reach the lower end of the Arizona Game and Fish land, bear left on the road; to reach the upper end, bear right about ¼ mile down Hatchery Way. You'll see a parking area for the upper end in about a mile or two. Fish downstream about ¼ to ½ mile below the parking area. If you go too far on this road you'll seen NO FISHING signs and a hatchery. All together there's more than a mile of good fishing. Some locals say that part or all of this stretch might eventually become catch-and-release—an excellent idea for Silver Creek.

The stream reminds me of an eastern limestone stream—but it certainly looks out of place in Arizona. It's a challenging, small, slow stream with plenty of high weeds lining the banks. A spring marks its headwaters, and you'll see the hatchery here, too. The stream warms in summer and consequently isn't stocked after May—but you will run into an occasional holdover.

In addition to the great little blue-winged olive dun hatch you'll find tricos on the water every day from June though September. Silver Creek empties into White Mountain Lake. Locals will tell you about some of the large rainbows that come out of this lake in spring to spawn.

BEST TIMES TO FISH THE HATCHES

April 1–May 31
Little Blue-Winged Olive Dun: afternoon, size 20
Speckle-Winged Dun: morning, size 16

June 1–September 30
Trico: morning, size 24
Little Blue-Winged Olive Dun: afternoon, size 20

SAN FRANCISCO RIVER

Rating: 5
Access: Good
Seasons: Sp, S, F
Maps: DeLorme p. 53; Apache National Forest map
Positives: Easy access, easy casting, good fishing just below Luna Lake
Negatives: Very small stream

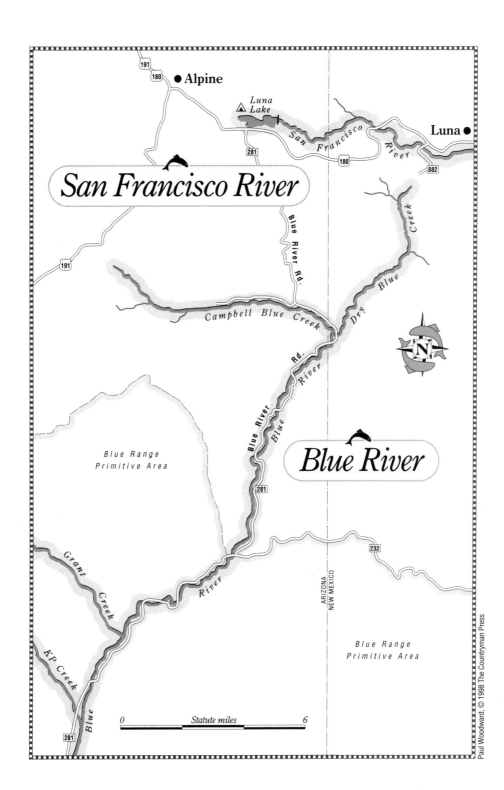

191
180
● Alpine

Luna
Lake

San Francisco River

San Francisco River

281
180

Luna ●

882

Blue River Rd.

Blue Creek

191

Campbell Blue Creek

Dry Blue

N

Blue River Rd.

Blue River

Blue River

Blue Range
Primitive Area

281

232

Grant Creek

River

ARIZONA
NEW MEXICO

Blue Range
Primitive Area

KP Creek

Blue

281

0   Statute miles   6

Luna Lake near Alpine

Bob Tulk fly-fishes the San Francisco River quite frequently; his favorite stretch is just upriver from the New Mexico border, where he fishes for some of the rainbow trout that make their way downriver from Luna Lake.

Ask Sonny Richards of Alpine about the San Francisco River, too. He'll probably show you a black Woolly Bugger type of fly that he swears takes lunkers here. The San Francisco River is only 15 feet wide. It has some deep runs and pools, and holds a fairly good trico hatch.

The San Francisco River begins just above Alpine, flows into Luna Lake, then out into New Mexico. You can catch trout as far downriver as the town of Luna, New Mexico. To reach the river in Arizona travel east on US 180 to Luna Lake. Turn left at the lake and follow this road to the outflow. Reach the river in New Mexico by taking US 180 to Forest Road (FR) 882; follow FR 882 ½ mile to the river.

Best Times to Fish the Hatches

April 1–May 31
Little Blue-Winged Olive Dun: afternoon, size 20

June 1–September 30
Black Quill: afternoon, size 14
Trico: morning, size 24
Little Blue-Winged Olive Dun: afternoon, size 20

BLUE RIVER

Rating: 6
Access: Fair to Good
Seasons: Sp, S, F
Maps: DeLorme p. 61, Apache National Forest map
Regulations: A New Mexico fishing license is required for about
  2 miles of the upper end of this river
Positives: Easy casting, easy access, streambred browns, little fishing
  pressure
Negatives: Some private land, no longer stocked

Look at the Blue River in far eastern Arizona in late April and you'd swear you're on any of a hundred small trout streams in Montana. It has easy access, plenty of productive riffles, and little fishing pressure.

Does it hold trout? Ask Dink Robarts of nearby Alpine. Dink's family owns a ranch on the Blue River, and Dink has seen 21-inch browns and 22-inch rainbows taken out of that stream. He'll also tell you that the upper end of the Blue holds some streambred brown trout. But the Blue and other northeastern Arizona trout streams have fallen on hard times. The state is not presently stocking this stream, in an effort to preserve the spinedace minnow. What a waste of a tremendous resource!

I fly-fished the upper Blue one late afternoon recently. I hit an area about 2 miles below the New Mexico boundary. The water was still running high from snowmelt in the high country. The Blue's an easy stream to fly-fish: You have plenty of open space to cast, and unlike most other rivers and streams in the Southwest, the Blue is relatively easy to reach. Take Blue River Road, which closely parallels the river, out of Alpine and you can be fishing within 35 minutes. Much of the Blue's upper end is in national forest. Even in high water and cold temperatures I managed to catch three streambred brown trout here.

There's a trout hatchery operated by Johnny Joy on the lower end of the Blue. Locals say that some of the big trout from this hatchery empty into the river. Way below Johnny Joy's place you'll find trout. Just ask Robert Tulk of Alpine: One day while fishing for catfish he landed a 17-inch rainbow in the Juan Miller Road area.

The Blue River is one of the few rivers in Arizona that boasts a gray drake hatch. You'll find these large mayflies appearing in early July in the afternoon. The Blue also holds some hellgrammites. A large, dark Woolly Bugger should copy these effectively.

The Blue holds plenty of pools and riffles and averages 20 to 25 feet in

The Blue River near the New Mexico border

width. It's easy to wade, and the scenery is no less than spectacular. The river begins where the Campbell Blue River joins the Dry Blue.

If you get the chance, try fishing one the productive tributaries of the Blue as well, like KP or Grant Creek. Both hold some good hatches (see hatch chart for Grant Creek below) and a lot of small rainbow trout. KP Creek drops about 3000 feet on its way to the Blue River.

BEST TIMES TO FISH THE HATCHES

April 1–May 31
Little Blue-winged Olive Dun: afternoon, size 20

June 1–September 30
Yellow Stonefly: evening, size 16
Dobson Fly: evening, size 6
Green Caddis: evening, size 14
Tan Caddis: evening, size 14 or 16
Gray Drake: afternoon, size 12
Trico: morning, size 24 (lower end)
Pale Evening Dun: evening,: size 16
Little Blue-Winged Olive Dun: afternoon, size 20

GRANT CREEK

BEST TIMES TO FISH THE HATCHES

April 15–May 31
Little Blue-Winged Olive Dun: afternoon, size 20
Quill Gordon: afternoon, size 16

June 1–September 30
Pale Evening Dun: evening, size 16
Dark Brown Dun: afternoon, size 14
Tan Caddis: evening, size 14 or 16

CAMPBELL BLUE CREEK

BEST TIMES TO FISH THE HATCHES

April 1–May 31
Little Blue-Winged Olive Dun: afternoon, size 20
Quill Gordon: afternoon, size 16
Pale Morning Dun: morning, size 16
Tan Caddis: evening, size 14 or 16

June 1–August 31
Pale Evening Dun: evening, size 16
Black Quill: afternoon, size 14
Trico: morning, size 24
Green Caddis: evening, size 14

September 1–October 31
Trico: morning, size 24
Little Blue-Winged Olive Dun: afternoon, size 20

SOUTH FORK OF NEGRITO CREEK

Rating: 8
Access: Good
Seasons: Sp, S, F
Maps: USGS Clifton
Regulations: A New Mexico fishing license is required
Positives: Easy access, large rainbow trout, some deep pools
Negatives: Small stream

I'll let you in on a secret gem of a stream if you promise to return every trout you catch. Let me explain in more detail.

On a recent fishing trip, just about every angler I met in Alpine, Arizona, and Reserve, New Mexico, suggested that I try fishing Willow Creek (see page 135)—a tributary of New Mexico's Gila River. It's 49 miles to Willow Creek from Reserve, and I had traveled just a little over halfway on Forest Road (FR) 435 when I got my first glimpse of another stream, the South Fork of Negrito Creek. This 15-foot-wide stream held many productive-looking deep pools, so I pulled in, parked the car, and assembled my gear. As I got closer to the stream, though, I started to doubt it held any good numbers of trout—it had an odd chalky blue color to it. But I tied on a Patriot dry fly with a Beadhead Pheasant Tail behind it.

The pool that I had selected was about 3 feet deep and 30 feet long. On my first cast a rainbow took the Beadhead after a 5-foot drift. I didn't land the fish, but it looked all of 15 inches long. On about my fifth cast another trout struck the Beadhead and the Patriot disappeared. This time I landed a dark red rainbow 18 inches long. Wow!

I then moved up to the next fairly deep pool and cast to an inviting riffle above. Again on my first cast, a trout hit the Beadhead and I missed it. On my second cast another trout hit, and I landed a 12-inch rainbow. Have you ever done so well somewhere that you began to wonder if maybe that stream was posted and you didn't see the signs?—or maybe that the season on that stream was closed? Both possibilities now entered my mind.

So I drove upstream another ½ mile to check for posters along the stream. When I pulled into a picnic area I couldn't resist—I began fishing again. A park ranger drove by, gave me a friendly wave, and left. I continued fly-fishing. I figured that if he'd seen me fishing and not stopped me, then the river must be open to fishing after all.

In that first pool in the picnic area I picked up three native rainbows that averaged about 5 inches long. This continued for the next hour. In two stops along the stream I figured I caught 15 to 20 rainbows—and nobody else was fishing!

South Fork of the Negrito Creek in New Mexico

Access to this stream is almost too easy—the forest road closely parallels it for about 4 miles. You'll find some little blue-winged olives and little brown stoneflies on the South Fork. This stream, especially in late April, is well worth a day of fly-fishing—even if you have to travel a couple hundred miles. But remember, you promised to return every fish you catch.

BEST TIMES TO FISH THE HATCHES

April 15–May 31
Little Blue-Winged Olive Dun: afternoon, size 20
Little Brown Stonefly: afternoon, size 16
Blue Quill: morning, size 18

June 1–September 30
Trico: morning, size 24 (spotty)
Tan Caddis: evening, size 14 or 16
Little Blue-Winged Olive Dun: afternoon, size 20

WILLOW CREEK

Rating: 6
Access: Good
Seasons: Sp, S, F
Maps: USGS Clifton
Regulations: A New Mexico fishing license is required
Positives: Easy access after a long drive
Negatives: Small stream, some sections difficult to fly-fish

What a trip—it takes 49 miles, mostly on dirt roads, to reach Willow Creek, a productive tributary of the Gila River. Once you arrive you'll see a 10- to 15-foot-wide, fast-flowing stream with plenty of rainbow trout. However, even late one recent April this high-altitude stream had snow along its banks. In fact, the road to the lower end of the stream was still closed by huge snowdrifts.

So I hiked along the stream's upper end, where little brown stoneflies were emerging in good numbers. I selected a section right along the road and began casting a Beadhead Pheasant Tail in the high, cloudy water. I didn't have to wait long—a small rainbow hit the wet fly on my fifth or sixth cast. I only landed a few small rainbows on Willow that morning, but I will return—when the waters recede.

To reach the stream take Forest Roads 435, 141, and 28, and follow the signs to Willow Creek. It's a long trip, so plan to stay overnight or start early in the morning. Will I return to Willow Creek? You'd better believe I will. Besides, I left my favorite Sage hat in Ella's Café in Reserve. I've got to get that back.

Best Times to Fish the Hatches

April 15–May 31
Little Blue-Winged Olive Dun: afternoon, size 20
Little Brown Stonefly: afternoon, size 16 or 18

June 1–September 30
Tan Caddis: evening, size 14 or 16
Trico: morning, size 24
Little Blue-Winged Olive Dun: afternoon, size 20

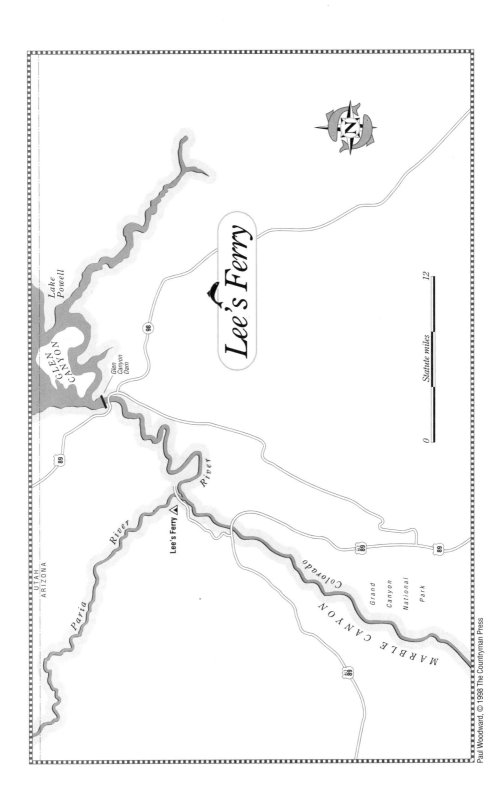

Lee's Ferry

Lake Powell

GLEN CANYON

Glen Canyon Dam

98

89

Paria River

River

UTAH
ARIZONA

Lee's Ferry

Colorado

MARBLE CANYON

Grand Canyon National Park

ALT 89

ALT 89

ALT 89

Statute miles

0   12

8

Lee's Ferry and the Colorado River

I can still remember my first trip up the Colorado from Lee's Ferry over 18 years ago. I knew immediately that I was in trouble with my wife—I'd fallen in love right away with the cold, clear, emerald green water, the bright red sandstone walls towering over 1000 feet straight up from the river, the feeling of being insignificant in the scheme of things . . . and I hadn't even rigged up my rod yet. I still get these feelings every time I head upriver and I'm sure I always will.

Lee's Ferry is managed as a trophy fishery. Barbless hooks are required. There's a no-kill slot limit of 16 to 22 inches, and you can keep two fish of less than 16 inches *or* one fish of less than 16 inches and one of over 22 inches.

LEE'S FERRY

Rating: 9
Access: Fair to Good
Seasons: Year-round
Maps: DeLorme p. 24
Regulations: Only artificial lures and flies with barbless hooks are allowed from Glen Canyon Dam to Marble Canyon Bridge in Coconino County
Positives: Big trout, year-round fishing, lodging and restaurant nearby
Negatives: Long drive from Phoenix

The story of the Lee's Ferry Fishery begins in June 1960, when the first bucket of concrete was poured into the 710-foot-high Glen Canyon Dam. A little over three years later this giant plug was permanently installed across Glen Canyon Gorge, and the beautiful, 186-mile-long Lake Powell was beginning to fill.

Glen Canyon Dam is a hydroelectric facility that produces power for the surrounding urban areas of California, Nevada, and Arizona. When the lake's 48-degree water was first released through the turbines and into the Colorado River below, Arizona Game and Fish realized the potential for a great tailwater fishery. Rainbow trout were planted in 1964 as catchables; they grew rapidly, and trout of over 10 pounds were soon common. Later, in 1976, a fingerling program was implemented to help sustain the desirable populations. Brookies and Lahontan cutthroats were released into the system from 1978 to 1980. These also attained great size—brookies up to 5 pounds and cutts over 7. Cutthroat stocking was discontinued in 1980, while brookies were planted until 1987. These fish were feeding mainly on scuds (*Gammarus lacustris,* planted in 1968 as a food source), *Chironomid,* and annelids (segmented aquatic worms). This is still the main diet of trout in the river, although in recent years, with constant higher-than-normal flows, midges have really taken hold to become a major portion of the trout's daily intake.

Water flows are determined by power demands and fluctuate daily as well as seasonally. They're at their lowest, around 13,000 cubic feet per second (cfs) in the morning; they start to rise around 9 AM to 22,000 cfs or more. (Flows usually run even higher in the heat of summer, when more power is needed to keep us city slickers cool.) As you can see, this is no little stream—it's a major waterway, with enough water volume to demand respect and caution while wading. When I first started fishing here years ago the fluctuations were even more drastic, and I was given some advice from Dr. Larry Allen that I never forgot. Larry was one of the fly-fishing pioneers of the Ferry back in the early 1980s, and truly one of the driving forces in the development of fly-fishing throughout Arizona. He told me to lay a $50 bill on a rock between myself and the shoreline off which I was fishing. Try it—I guarantee you'll keep a constant watch on the rising height of the water on that rock. I never had the spare $50 to try it myself, but I'm sure it would have worked. The point is to keep checking the water flows. Don't get yourself stranded out on a gravel bar with a deep channel to cross to get back to shore.

The river has had its share of problems, as have many tailwater fisheries in the West. I could give you all the details, but they are complex and make for dull reading. The troubles can be attributed mainly to the floods of

1983, increased angling pressure, and a series of stream-flow drawdowns that decimated the river's aquatic flora and fauna. Much of the *Cladophora* (the dominant weed growth) was lost, especially along the river's edges. This is the scud's main habitat, so the trout's main food source suffered greatly. Nematodes that were already present in the river system took hold of the weakened fish, and the original planted rainbows were lost. The nematode doesn't seem to affect healthy fish, but after the stress of spawning in the already decimated periphery of the river, the fish had a hard time recovering. Fishermen began catching snakelike fish with large heads and skinny bodies. Thus after several spawning seasons, as much as 50 percent of the fish were lost. Unfortunately, no records had been kept of the origins or even the strains of rainbows that were originally planted. Early stockings by Arizona Game and Fish were determined by the availability of healthy, inexpensive eggs, without concern for strain. Some had just a very few spots; others were totally covered, looking almost like the leopard trout of Alaska. Still, the fish all had thick bodies and broad shoulders, and they all exhibited great fight when hooked. They were excellent fish, and it's a shame they were lost.

Kamloops rainbows were planted in 1985 as marked fish and didn't fare well. They were discontinued in 1988 because of poor return-to-creel figures. The Bel Air rainbow has been the strain transplanted since then and is the dominant strain in the river today, with more naturally spawned fish being seen all the time. This is probably due to the higher stream flows in recent years, which give newly hatched fry a better chance of survival. The eggs are less likely to be eaten by predators or dry up on the high-and-dry gravel bars. Also, steady water levels don't break as much of the weed growth loose from the streambed, allowing more hiding places for young fish, and keeping redds safer from being trampled by fishermen. It would be a great day for us all if Lee's Ferry could be assured of enough stream flow to allow for successful spawns *every year*. I would love to see what characteristics would become dominant in a naturally spawned strain of rainbows.

The river has a 1½ mile stretch of wadable river below the Lee's Ferry boat ramps. This is good water with decent numbers of fish, mostly in the 14- to 16-inch range, with some larger fish showing up during the spawn. Often these trout can be taken on top when the midges are coming off. (I've never been able to take fish on top unless they're already actively midging.) This can be particularly exciting fishing. To date, almost 37 different midge species have been documented on the river, some as small as size 26. At times, the fish can be especially particular about the size, color, or placement of a fly—it should be floating in the film or right on top, especially when the hatch is prolific. Maintaining a good drag-free drift is also important. Most of the time the fish won't move far to take your fly. There are so many naturals coming off, none of which represents much of a meal, that a fish won't move out of its lane to get one. Luckily most of this fishing is done close in, making it easier for you to keep track of your tiny fly and to cast precisely.

A good fly choice is often a large dry, such as a Royal Wulff or Adams Irresistible, used as an indicator, with a midge trailing close behind. My fishing buddy Steve Kelly uses a Disco Midge as his trailer and is always into fish with it. This is an especially good tactic in fairly shallow water. The same setup can be used in deeper water with a small weighted midge, scud, or worm pattern, and a longer tippet. Just make sure the weight is not so heavy that it sinks your indicator fly. Most of the time you'll be using anywhere from one split shot to two BBs, depending on the water flow and depth you're fishing. As you walk a gravel bar or the bank you're fishing, you may have to change the depth of your fly. You'll catch these fish right above the bottom or close to the top when they're actively midging; you won't catch many middepth. I like to use poly floating yarn as my indicator, using different colors under different light conditions. Fluff it up, add some floatant before fishing, and it will usually last all day, depending on how many times you're lucky enough to watch it go under. If it doesn't ride right on top, make a few false casts to disperse as much water as possible and reapply more paste floatant—you'll be back in business. The higher your indicator rides, the better it will work. Sometimes the take is nothing more than a slight hesitation or a faint turn in the indicator. If your indicator is not right on top, you'll have a harder time recognizing these delicate takes.

Most fishing is done in the 15 miles upriver. I recommend that on your first trip upriver, you use a guide or go with someone who has knowledge of the winding river channel. Although higher flows make boating safer, gravel bars still take their toll on the inexperienced boater. At several places, the river must be negotiated through its main channel or you'll be taking your prop to the repair shop on your trip home. (It's wise to have an extra prop and shear pins on board.) There are several guide outfits on the river that provide excellent service to novice and expert alike. Their large, enclosed, shallow-draft river boats with heaters are a real comfort in winter (see page 144 for names and addresses).

A common practice is to boat upriver and beach on a gravel bar. Fishing the edges of these bars, the riffles at the top, and tailouts and backwaters is productive at times. During the spawn, sight fishing is common and very productive. Higher flows in recent years have cost us a few fishing spots on

A rainbow caught at Lee's Ferry

the river; at times, the fishermen may outnumber the available fishing areas. Take a break and enjoy the scenery, or try for some of the midging fish in the scum lines in the main river. Usually fishermen are considerate enough not to hog a spot all day. If a spot doesn't open up, slowly motor up to the resident group and see if you may be able to share the lower or upper end of the bar. Common courtesy is always appreciated.

For equipment, I recommend a 9- or 9½-foot rod for 5- or 6-weight with enough backbone to throw some split shot. Longer rods make mending line easier. At times, a fish will follow your fly downstream and you may need an extended drift to coax it into taking. Indeed, sometimes this technique is essential, but I've never been an advocate of long drifts. Line control is difficult when you have large amounts of line out, and your percentage of hooking and landing fish will be diminished, especially if you're using a smaller fly—and most anglers here do use small flies, in sizes 20 through 14, with some kind of weight to get them down. Remember, scuds, worms, eggs (during the spawn), and the larval stage of *Chironomid* are the patterns most often used. These are all fished right above the bottom. Many can be tied with beadheads to help get them to the desired level.

For my first day on this river I usually rig up two flies, with split shot about 10 inches above the top fly. I want to determine what the fish are keying on that day; two flies makes it easier and faster for me to figure it out. And even if I have a good idea of what they're taking, their preferences can vary at times or in certain areas of the river, and I still need to know what color, what size? Once I determine the predominant fly of the day, I usually cut back to just that fly. I don't know why, but I find it more enjoyable fooling fish with one fly. I guess it makes me feel I'm a little more in tune with the fish.

In addition to my large rod, I always have a 4-weight rigged with a 6X fluorocarbon tippet for the midging trout I encounter on this river. This is the most gratifying kind of fly-fishing to me. Fish congregate at certain areas of the river in the scum lines or breaks behind boulders. Depending on the water flow, you may find numbers of fish behind the gravel bars in shallow stillwater feeding on midge adults or spinners. This is the most technical form of fly-fishing at the Ferry. Yes, it can be frustrating and fruitless, but it's always fun.

The river temperature hovers around the 48-degree mark, year-round, so neoprene waders are a good investment. The newer breathable waders have become popular with the local guides. Although comfortable, they don't provide warmth, so you need warm clothing as well. Layering with some sort of wickable material against your skin works best. How much layering you need depends on your tolerance for the cold. The canyon walls are very high upstream, and many areas of the river don't receive sunlight in winter. It can be extremely cold if you're going upriver at 30 miles per hour on a morning when the thermometer reads 10 degrees! I can remember the first time I took my dad upstream here; it was January. I always try to fish shady water—I find that fish are more cooperative there. My dad kept saying, "I don't care. Get me in the sun!" It was a never-ending battle, with us usually fishing in the sun.

Although Lee's Ferry can be fished year-round, the fishery has different characteristics in the different seasons. The rainbows here are rather unique in that they spawn in fall. Bright-colored 'bows can begin to show up in the shallows as early as October in preparation for the spawn. This is the busiest time of the year on the river; your chances of catching the largest rainbow you've ever caught are increased during the spawn, and everybody realizes it. As fish move into the shallow gravel areas to begin their survival ritual, they become more accessible. Sight fishing is the usual technique employed during this time. Polarized sunglasses are a must to spot the trout on the redds. *If you can spot the trout before it spots you, you're at a great advantage.* Drifting egg patterns through the trout's territory is the most successful tactic during this time. Keep a low profile around shallow water, cast upstream with minimal false casts, and maintain a good dead drift through each area—this will usually put you into fish. Again, make sure you have enough weight to get your fly down into the trout's window of vision. These fish usually won't move far to grab your offering. I have found that when fishermen are doing everything right, but aren't hooking up, they usually don't have the fly down in the fish's face.

Many fishermen shy away from fishing the spawn, and I have to admit I have my concerns, too. I try not to fish a pair that are actively spawning, I'm careful with each trout while releasing it. I try not to even handle the fish. I don't use a net, and most of the time I can simply reach down, grab the barbless hook, turn it upside down, and the fish is gone . . . hopefully to continue its main objective, reproduction. These fish are the future of the river. If we all treat them with respect and a little TLC, we'll be able to enjoy them longer.

After the stress of spawning, which may last well into spring, the fish return to their normal lives and resume their daily feeding habits. This is a great time of year to be on the water. Fish are feeding vigorously, trying to rejuvenate themselves after the rigors of reproduction. The weather is wonderful, and the midges begin to hatch with daily regularity. Deep-water nymphing for the fish in the deeper runs or below dropoffs and gravel bars becomes the most commonly used technique. Top-water midging is also a possibility, so keep your eyes peeled for telltale noses poking through the surface in the eddies and backwaters.

Summer months usually mean higher flows, due to the increased power demands from urban areas for air-conditioning. It also means *very* hot weather on the river. If you can handle the heat, you can enjoy some of the best top-water fishing of the year. Midge hatches continue, joined by occasional hopper activity below brushy areas on the riverbanks. It's a thrill to see an aggressive take on a hopper—trout do not sip them! At the start of the hopper season, it's always a challenge to me to actually hook a trout. I generally need a few missed takes before I remember I have to let the fish take the fly *and turn away* before I yank the "meal" out of its mouth.

I'm always anxious for the end of summer and the beginning of cooler weather. Fall will find me back on the river, waiting for that first red-cheeked rainbow to show up in the shallows.

As I mentioned earlier, this river can be hazardous—hire a guide for your first visit, or at least go with someone who knows the river. There are excellent guides here, with boats specially designed to traffic this river's shallow waters. These guides are on the water every day and will most certainly give you your best chance at catching the rainbow of your dreams.

I have recommended many anglers to two outfits in particular and have never heard a complaint. Dave Foster and his wife, Barbara, run the Marble Canyon Guide Service (1-800-533-7339). I also recommend Dave's book, *The Lee's Ferry*—the most comprehesive, informative book on the river. And Terry and Wendy Gunn run Lee's Ferry Anglers (1-800-962-9755). They also operate a nearby, fully stocked fly shop that can help you with all of your fly-fishing needs.

There are several lodgings available close to the river, including the Marble Canyon Lodge (1-800-726-1789); Lee's Ferry Lodge (520-355-2231); and Cliffdweller (1-800-433-2543). All three offer reasonable rates, a restaurant, and gas. Sack lunches can be made for your next day's fishing.

Lee's Ferry is a 4½- to 5-hour drive north from Phoenix. Take Interstate 17 to Flagstaff, then head north on US 89 to US 89A. It's a 14-mile drive on 89A to the Navajo Bridge, where you'll get your first glimpse of the Colorado. On the west side of the bridge you'll see signs for the Ferry, the campground and parking areas. Don't be alarmed if the water looks like chocolate; the Paria River dumps into the Colorado below the Ferry and can discolor the river if there have been recent rains up in Utah. The first time I saw this river, I was totally panicked—I thought I'd have to catch trout in chocolate milk. But when I made it to the water's edge, the river was the emerald green I had envisioned. It's always clear, even after heavy rains. That's one of the beauties of tailwaters—they are always fishable and full of big trout. I'm thankful to have this one so close to my home, and plan to fish it for many more years to come.

BEST TIMES TO FISH THE HATCHES

April 1–September 30
Little Blue-Winged Olive Dun: afternoon, size 20
Chironomid: morning, sizes 20–26

9

Arizona's High Lakes

Much of this book has been devoted to Arizona's trout streams and rivers—but it wouldn't be complete without a chapter on our fine still-water fishing. By far, most of the trout fishing in Arizona is done on the high lakes. All the lakes I'll discuss here are above the Mogollon Rim in central Arizona; they range in elevation from 7000 feet, around Williams, to over 9000 feet in the White Mountains. Their diverse regions offer many opportunities to catch the states' rainbows, native Apaches, browns, brookies, cutthroats, and grayling. Depending on the severity of the winter, some of these lakes can actually be fished almost year-round. You'll learn to appreciate this if, after a day on the water in December, you watch the evening news and see what the weather's like up north. You know the folks up there didn't enjoy the day like you did!

I'll divide this discussion of the lakes into two regions: the Mogollon Rim and the White Mountains. As you head eastward along the Rim, you'll gain altitude until you reach what I consider the prettiest part of our state, the White Mountains. This region is heavily forested with pon-derosa, fir, spruce, and aspen trees, and has the most opportunities for trout fishing in both lakes and streams. Anyone seeing it for the first time would not believe that two hours down the road are saguaro cactus.

It must be noted that all these lakes depend almost entirely on runoff from the previous season's snowpack. Although it's easy to forget while on any of these lakes, Arizona *is* a desert state, and water is definitely a precious commodity here. Water quality, and consequently the quality of the fishing, is affected by the amount of nutrients that enter the lake through runoff in spring. Recent winters in Arizona have been mild, with little snowpack in the

RON DUNGAN

Sunrise Lake

mountains. A few of the lakes with no stream inflow became dangerously low and actually suffered some kill at the end of summer in 1997. This will happen with some regularity in Arizona. It's rare when a lake that fishes well one year is the best lake again the following year.

The reason for this is that when a lake gets low, more weeds grow, and occupy more space in the available water. This can affect the water's pH, causing fish to suspend feeding. Some lakes also get so weedy that it's difficult to launch a float tube and get out to where the water is fishable. With more weeds, the fish have more cover and become harder to find. Weeds also create problems in presenting your fly properly. It's not so much that the fish aren't there, it's just much harder to get your fly in front of them.

Still, one advantage to weed growth is the structure it provides for the trout. I use a fish finder on my float tube and I inevitably find that the larger fish are right up against the weeds or in the pockets where there's cover and plenty of food. At times all I need to catch fish is to be able to place my fly in the pocket. A good cast almost ensures a hookup. I'm not sure whether the fish are there for the cover, or because they're feeding on the insects in the weeds. It really doesn't really matter, though; when they're there, more often than not they're feeding.

The lakes are open to fishing year-round, but for the reasons I've mentioned, you'll find the best conditions in spring and fall.

THE WHITE MOUNTAINS

White Mountain lakes can be divided into two groups—those located on Indian reservations (White Mountain Apache and San Carlos Apache) and those in the national forests. The lakes on the reservations are managed by the respective tribes and require a daily license to fish ($5). No state license is required. Camping and boating fees are extra, and some of the lakes carry a special use designation, with special permits required for each. Check with your local fly shop to determine which licenses or permits are needed.

National forest lakes require a state fishing license and a trout stamp. Arizona has some good programs for nonresident licensing—a one-day license costs $8.50, a five-day license $18.50, and a four-month license $22. Trout stamps are not needed with these licenses. Residents pay $12 for a fishing license and $10 for the trout stamp. The proceeds from trout stamps go to fund our trout hatcheries.

RESERVATION LAKES

SUNRISE LAKE

Rating: 8
Access: Good
Seasons: Year-round
Maps: DeLorme p. 53, White Mountain Apache maps
Positives: Strong-fighting trout, good damsel hatch, various species
 of trout, marina, boat rentals
Negatives: Often winterkill, windy in spring, weedy at season's end

Sunrise Lake was created in the mid-1960s and covers an area of 700 to 900 acres, depending on the year; at 9100 feet, this lake is the largest and one of the highest on the White Mountain Apache Reservation. It's also (in my opinion) the most fertile, and has consistently produced big, hard-fighting rainbows and brookies in the past. It's part of the Snake Creek drainage and is rather shallow, especially on its southern end. There's not a lot of water feeding the lake from Snake Creek, so (as you will hear many times), the lake depends on spring runoff from the surrounding hills and mountains to the west. In the past few years, the lake has suffered from low runoff. It lost the majority of its brook trout in 1997 due to low pH in late summer. The rainbows made it through the

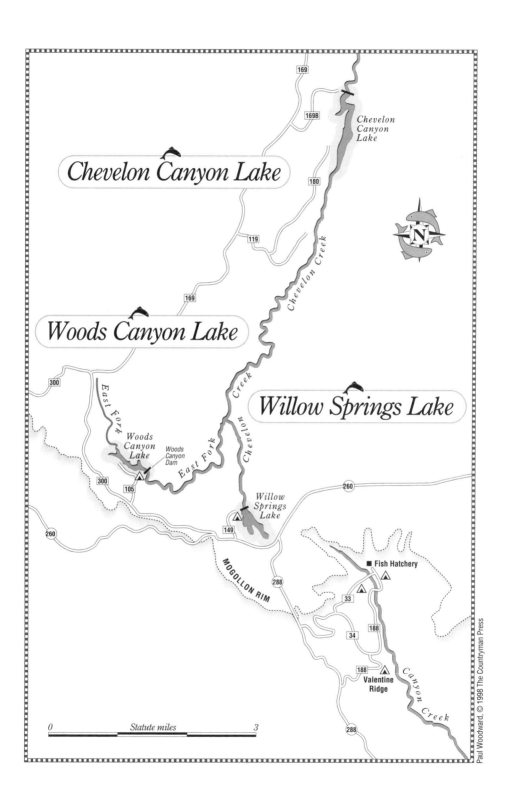

Chevelon Canyon Lake

Woods Canyon Lake

Willow Springs Lake

169

169B

Chevelon
Canyon
Lake

180

Chevelon Creek

119

169

East Fork

300

Woods
Canyon
Lake

Woods
Canyon
Dam

East Fork Creek

Chevelon Creek

300

105

260

Willow
Springs
Lake

260

149

MOGOLLON RIM

288

Fish Hatchery

33

188

34

188

188

Valentine
Ridge

Canyon Creek

288

0   Statute miles   3

Paul Woodward, © 1998 The Countryman Press

poor conditions, however, and were extremely healthy and strong that summer, although hard to catch; the low pH slowed their feeding. Still, these rainbows are Erwin strain—a fairly long-living strain from Ennis, Montana—and have grown to over ten pounds in hatchery conditions. They were stocked in Sunrise after the winterkill of 1992–93.

In 1997 I landed several of these trout over 21 inches long and 4 pounds. I was also broken off numerous times using 3x tippet. In fact, I was fishing with Don Carlson when I was broken off three times in one day; my "good friend" thought this quite funny. I generally fish leech patterns very slowly in an up-and-down motion. These fish broke me off on the bottom of the stroke; I never even had a chance to set the hook. After the third one hit me like a freight train, I was so mad I just about threw my rod in the lake. As I look back, it was a nice problem to have had. I hope this strain is replanted in the lake.

Sunrise has rainbows, brookies, some grayling, and native Apache trout; the dominant fish depends on the previous winter's snowpack. The different species coexist compatibly and allow for good season-long fishing. The rainbows can be caught at ice-out while they try to spawn along the rocky edges, and will still take a fly during the warmer months of summer. The brookies are best in spring and again in fall when they're stacked up trying to spawn. Apaches really slow down in the heat of summer, but earlier and later in the season are your best candidates for top-water action when the *Baetis* and *Callibaetis* come off. You'll always find a few trout midging during the season, but it can be difficult to actually fish a hatch here— they're usually very sporadic. The action is cast-and-wait.

Still, at times there are sufficient *Callibaetis* coming off to warrant putting on an emerger and casting to cruising feeders. This doesn't happen often during the season, but can really be fun when the opportunity arises. It's always wise to have some Blue-Winged Olives in sizes 16 to 20 in both dry and emerger patterns. The same is true with *Callibaetis:* Carry Speckle-Winged Duns in sizes 14 to 18. Generally an Adams will work fine. I prefer the parachute style because of the way it rides in the water. The body rides low in the film, and the parachute hackle resembles a mayfly's legs extending over the water. Also, the little white post is nice for those of us with older eyes.

But the dominant hatch here each season is the damsel. This usually occurs in early June, depending on the weather and water conditions. This is an exciting hatch to fish, with many fish taken either on top or just under the surface. The damsels live in the lake's weed beds; to hatch they swim to shore and climb above the surface on the first object they find. Many never make it to a suitable perch and simply hatch right there on the mud.

After the hatch starts, you'll see the shoreline littered with discarded shucks. As the damsels swim to shore you'll see them coming toward you, some actually climbing onto your float tube to hatch and then, in a few minutes, fly away. (I often leave this lake with shucks on my hat from the lucky damsels that made it up my neck and onto my head without getting swatted and sent to damsel heaven.) Many swim to shore on the surface or just below it, but many others come to shore deeper in the water column. These latter damsel nymphs swim in a wiggling motion and pretty much parallel to the bottom (unlike mayfly nymphs or caddis, which will emerge with an upward motion). They can be imitated by using a full-sinking line, which allows you to present your fly more naturally.

Let me share with you the way I fish Sunrise or any other lake with a damsel hatch in progress. First, I like to be on the water before daylight. I rig up in the dark. Usually the damsels start coming off around 9 or 10 AM, but that doesn't mean the fish aren't already feeding on something else. Many times the bigger fish will come into the shallows during the night to feed on leeches, scuds, mayfly nymphs, and any other edible goodies they can find. These fish feel more secure in the dark and will come in shallower to feed. At times, if sunrise is just starting and you're in the right position, you can see the backs of feeding fish. Put on a floating line and cast to the nearest trout. *Don't get in the water.* If none are visible, cast blindly to just in front of the weed beds. Fish are often found in this shallower water, waiting for the damsels to start their migration to shore. You probably won't catch a lot of fish this way, but the ones you do will be nice. The fight can be dramatic—in shallow water, trout either leap straight up or run like a bonefish . . . fun! Once you catch a few good fish in this shallow water, though, it spooks the rest. After you've worked your area thoroughly, get in your float tube and head out to the weed beds, which are the nursery for the aquatic insect life in the lake. Before the sun hits the water, trout will cruise over the tops of the weeds and feed on the available insect life. Get right out in the middle of the weeds and spray-cast in a circle to every area you can reach. Try to make as little commotion as possible—keep your casts to a minimum, especially your false casts. Again, you may see feeding trout, and this is always a bonus. Although you're in deeper water now, the fish are in relatively shallow water over the tops of the weeds and will be aware of any object that wasn't there earlier. After the sun hits the water, the trout generally drop off the outer edge of the weeds and can be fished more conventionally with your sinking line. This is where I head if I can't get on the water as early as I like. Fish will feed along these edges during the day, then return to the shallows as darkness approaches. The cycle starts all over again.

Using these techniques, you can find and fish for trout effectively during the whole day. This doesn't mean you'll *catch* fish all day—after all, they're still fish and definitely have minds of their own. But at least you'll be presenting your fly to them in a natural manner.

Recently Kelly Meyer, the fisheries biologist for White Mountain Apache Game and Fish, gave me a copy of the tribe's four- or five-year *proposed* plan. Under this proposal Sunrise will be managed as a trophy lake, with emphasis on improving its water quality, cutting down the weeds prior to winter freezeup, and fencing off the northern end of the lake to keep cattle from entering. (Excrement from the cattle encourages weed growth, adding to the problem of winterkill.) Part of the problem of supplying badly needed fresh water every spring may be addressed by fixing a drainage pipe from a catchment lake on Mount Baldy (the mountain from which Sunrise receives most of its runoff every spring). Weed cutting will decrease the chance of winterkill each year and improve the survival rate of the larger fish over the long winter months. These larger fish are affected by low oxygen levels more severely than smaller ones, and are usually the first to die. Usually the lake freezes over around early December and opens around early April, so there are four months without open water for the trout to contend with. If we can improve the quality of the water before freezeup and reduce the amount of weeds decomposing in the lake, we'll better our chances of catching that trout we've been dreaming about.

Sunrise can be reached by taking AZ 260 east from Pinetop to AZ 273. Turn south on 273; you'll reach the lake in approximately 4 miles. There's a 100-room hotel at the lake complete with a restaurant, a marina with boat rentals available, and a small general store that offers gas, groceries, fishing gear, flies, and fishing permits.

Be sure to give Sunrise a try when you're in the White Mountains. Check the local fly shops to find out what's working best, and get ready for some of the hardest-fighting rainbows you'll find anywhere.

RESERVATION LAKE

Rating: 6
Access: Good
Seasons: Year-round
Maps: DeLorme p. 53, White Mountain Apache maps
Positives: No crowds, abundant wildlife, scenic
Negatives: Long drive from town along a maze of dirt roads

If fly-fishing in a crowd diminishes the pleasure of your experience, Reservation may be the lake for you, especially in spring and fall. Getting here requires a rather lengthy drive on the southern side of Mount Baldy. And the lake lies right up against the boundary of the Mount Baldy Wilderness Area, the stronghold of the great White Mountain Apache elk herd. This area is off limits to any nontribal member during the year, unless you have deep enough pockets to afford their pricey elk hunt in the fall. This is prime summer range for the elk, and there are always lots in the area during the fishing season. If you hit the lake late in fall you'll hear bulls bugling all around you during the day. Then, as the light begins to fade in the evening, you can usually get a glimpse of one coming out of the timber. It's an incredible sight that I look forward to every fall.

Last October I was with my fishing partner Dave Wilder on the backside of the lake. It had been cold the night before—about 12 degrees—the wind had been blowing, and we were camping out. (I keep trying to convince Dave that he is old, like me, and should be sleeping in a warm bed every night. It hasn't worked yet.) The water was numbing, with our guides freezing up after every second cast, and the fishing had been moderate at best. The only thing going through my mind was, "What the heck am I doing out here freezing?" Just then a huge six-point bull came out of the timber not 70 yards from me, and looked right at me in my float tube. He laid back his big rack and let out the loudest bellow I've ever heard; it continued for about three minutes. It made my whole day worthwhile. You may not realize it, but in Arizona you can see tremendous amounts of game while traveling the backwoods or fishing the lakes and streams. On an average trip into Reservation Lake you'll see elk, deer, turkey, grouse, and possibly a bear. This makes even slow fishing days memorable.

Constructed in 1964, Reservation is the highest lake on the White Mountain Apache Reservation and also one of the most remote. Roads into the lake are usually snowbound by the end of November, and usually won't be cleared until April. It lies in the Black River drainage and is fed by Reservation Creek, which comes off Mount Baldy. This consistent inflow is one of the major reasons that winterkill is not a problem on Reservation. It is shaped much like a V with two distinct arms, one running north and the other westerly. The former is fed by Reservation Creek; you'll find some browns up in the top end during the fall spawning season. In recent years I've seen fewer browns, however—possibly because the upper end of the lake is silting up from runoff and not as many spawning fish are returning in the shallow water. A 1995 fire on the south side of Mount Baldy may be contributing to the erosion problem upstream.

The lake has a good population of rainbows and brookies. Native

Apache trout were planted as far back as 1989, but have not adapted to the lake as well as expected. The western arm of the lake is a little deeper, with a few more coves and some deeper drop-offs. It also is larger and, in the past few years, has fished better than the northern arm. The lake does not have many aquatic weeds, which has both good and bad points. The lack of weeds means fewer aquatic insects and, consequently, fewer hatches. But it also means that the lake doesn't suffer alga blooms during the hot summer months, and you can usually depend on finding a gorgeous body of water when you head to Reservation. Because of the lack of insects, trout prey more on crayfish, leeches, and smaller fish. This may explain why browns seem to do so well in the lake. I usually use big Buggers or streamers here, with a Peacock Lady trailer, on a full-sinking line. In the early season and late fall I use a type II line; I switch to faster-sinking type IV in the heat of summer to get down where the big boys are.

Reservation offers good camping areas all around its southern and western sides. A small marina with boat rentals is open usually from Memorial Day to Labor Day, and tribal permits are available at the store. (If you make it into the lake in early spring or late fall, make sure you purchase your permit in town.) Although the scenery is beautiful, you'll have a long drive in before you can wet a line. Reservation Lake can be reached by taking Indian Route 55 east from Whiteriver all the way to Indian Route 8. Head north until you hit the lake.

HORSESHOE CIENEGA LAKE

Rating: 6
Access: Good
Seasons: Year-round
Maps: DeLorme p. 53, White Mountain Apache map
Positives: Easy to get to, can be fished when windy
Negatives: Does get crowded, lots of smaller trout

Horseshoe Cienega Lake is in the Bog Creek drainage and is fed by a diversion ditch from Bog Creek. This is one reason why it's not in much danger of winterkill. It fishes much like Sunrise and, like that lake, is characterized by heavy patches of weeds in the warmer months of summer. It features abundant insect life—indeed, it's your best opportunity for dry-fly fishing on the reservation. *Baetis* and *Callibaetis* are the major mayfly hatches, and a number of ant hatches come off with amazing regularity as well. At least one of the species of ant is so small that, unless you look closely, you'll think it's a midge hatch. I once fooled a few fish with a size 20 midge emerger.

On Horseshoe Cienega Lake

Most of the fish you'll catch here will be smaller, but the damselfly hatch is a different story. Horseshoe Cienega Lake has good numbers of damsels and is one of the few lakes where top-water damsel action is predictable. Large browns and rainbows can be caught using floating lines with both damsel adult and damsel nymph imitations. When the trout are feeding top water on damsels, the trick is not to spook them. If you position yourself and your tube in a cove or along a weed bed with fish taking spent damsels or hatching nymphs, try not to kick around. The bigger fish will pick up on the movement in the water and discontinue feeding. It can be a little nerve racking and you have to have some patience, but your best strategy is just to wait until one begins feeding, then cast your imitation in its direction. I've caught some of my largest rainbows and browns this way in Horseshoe Cienega Lake.

This lake is one that can still be fished when the wind blows you off Sunrise, or any other lake located out in the open. More than once I've been unable to fish Sunrise because of the wind—but headed just down the road to Horseshoe and could actually dry-fly fish. One time in particular, my fishing buddies Jack Morales, Doug Esquivel, Don Carlson, and I had been on a marathon jaunt. We'd started well before daylight and hit three lakes by midafternoon. The wind and 3-foot whitecaps made Sunrise unfishable, so we came down to Horseshoe. When we hit the parking lot we were was so exhausted that we just sat in our trucks and watched the lake. No one was anxious to get out and launch the float tubes. But after several minutes someone saw a rise out in front of us—then saw another one and then another—and before you knew it, there were four weary-looking fishermen heading to the water's edge. We just sat down on the edge of the lake and cast little parachute Adams until dark. I don't know how many fish we caught, but I remember that a couple of them were nice browns. We probably didn't look very distinguished sitting on our behinds, but we sure had fun.

Horseshoe Cienega Lake offers good camping sites on its southern side. The grocery store and marina are open from Memorial Day to Labor Day, and permits can be purchased there. Rental boats are available; boaters do well trolling Buggers or damsel imitations along the edges of the weeds.

Horseshoe Cienega Lake produced the state-record brown trout—over 17 pounds. The lake was renovated in 1990 to thin out its weeds and remove unwanted sunfish. It's been many years now since the lake was replanted . . . which should be long enough for a brown to grow to at least 17½ pounds.

EARL PARK LAKE

Rating: 7
Access: Good
Seasons: Year-round
Maps: DeLorme p. 52, White Mountain Apache maps
Positives: Catch-and-release; large Apache, rainbow, and brown
    trout; good size for float-tubing; great scenery
Negatives: Needs better monitoring—fish are being taken

Earl Park Lake is a small lake, about 47 acres, and is the White Mountain Apache Reservation's first catch-and-release lake. It's also one of the prettiest I've ever seen. It's tucked in behind Hawley Lake, only ½ mile from the store and marina, but even with such close proximity to one of the busiest lakes in the state, Earl Park receives little pressure. It's fed from the east by the headwaters of Trout Creek. This constant inflow and the depth of the lake help maintain good fishing conditions here during the summer months, even when drought conditions occur in the state. Several years ago, after three years of drought, this lake fished well all through summer and into fall. Recently, however, fish numbers have declined due to poaching. The tribe is well aware of the problem and is making every effort to put an end to it.

On Earl Park Lake

The lake has big browns, rainbows, brookies, and some very nice Apaches that are eager to take a dry fly in the evening. Earl Park is nestled into a basin west of the closed area of the Mount Baldy Wilderness and is sheltered from the winds, which generally come from the west. No facilities are available lakeside, but Hawley Lake, 10 minutes away, offers lodging, great campsites, food, gas, and permits. Earl Park can be reached by taking AZ 473 off AZ 260. The road is paved to within a few miles of Hawley, and is one of the prettier drives in Arizona. With any luck you'll get a glimpse of the abundant wildlife here, too: Deer, elk, turkey, and bear are common sights on the 11-mile drive up the hill to Hawley. Indeed, this lake is worth the time for the drive alone.

CYCLONE, HURRICANE, AND CHRISTMAS TREE LAKES

Rating: 8
Access: Good
Seasons: Year-round
Maps: DeLorme p. 53, White Mountain Apache map
Positives: Good places to find solitude, holds brood-stock Apache trout

Negatives: Fishing slows during warm weather

I've grouped these lakes together because they're all managed as special permit lakes; the number of anglers allowed on the water daily is limited. Christmas Tree is managed on a first-come, first-served basis, and Hurricane and Cyclone are managed on the rent-a-lake program. Permits can be obtained from the White Mountain Apache Game and Fish in Whiteriver by calling (520) 338-4385 or 338-4386. Each lake has a different price and/or program; check with the department for details. These lakes are good choices for large groups of friends, family get-togethers, or businesses that want to enjoy some fishing with a little privacy.

All three lakes are stocked during the season with Apache trout brood stock from the Williams Creek Hatchery in Whiteriver. This is your best chance to catch one of Arizona's trophy native trout. Apaches are the dominant species in all three lakes, although there's a good population of holdover browns in Christmas Tree and some nice rainbows in Cyclone. The tribe would like to eliminate the browns from Christmas Tree and have set liberal bag limits accordingly.

All three of these lakes are rather small—from 20 to 50 acres—and can easily be fished from a float tube or boat. Hurricane and Cyclone have

Fishing Camp at Cyclone Lake

Cyclone Lake

little vegetation, and crawfish are abundant in both. Christmas Tree is quite the opposite, with weeds becoming quite dense as summer nears. This makes for good damsel habitat and the Apaches will take both nymphs and adults when the damsel hatch is under way, usually in June. *Callibaetis* is the major mayfly, and a Pheasant Tail or Hare's Ear serves as a good imitation. An Adams or parachute Adams is all you need when the hatch is under way. My favorite setup for Christmas Tree is a Damsel Nymph with a soft-hackle Pheasant Tail trailer fished on an intermediate or slow-sinking line, depending on the stage of the emergence. (Of course, this is true of any lake with damsels and mayflies in the early season.) As summer warms the water and the trout go deeper, I generally switch over to a type III or IV sinking line, and I fish buggers or leeches slowly using short intermittent strips with pauses to let the fly fall. Most takes are at the bottom of the pause, just as I start to lift the fly.

Christmas Tree Lake is reached from Whiteriver by taking Indian Route 55 east to Route 60. Drive on Route 60 north about 10–15 miles. Follow signs to the lake. You can get to Cyclone Lake by taking Route 473 for about 2 miles around Hawley Lake and then following marked signs for another 5 or 6 miles. Hurricane Lake can be reached by taking Indian Route 55 east from Whiteriver all the way to Indian Route 8. It's about 5 miles before Reservation Lake.

Give these lakes a thought the next time you're getting together a large group—or fish them by yourself. They're all good lakes, especially early in the season.

NATIONAL FOREST LAKES

BIG LAKE

Rating: 7
Access: Good
Seasons: Year-round
Maps: DeLorme p. 53, White Mountain Apache maps
Positives: Good campgrounds, boat rentals, general store and
    marina, beautiful scenery
Negatives: Gets crowded in summer

Big Lake is the crown jewel of the national forest lakes and is used by more outdoorsmen than any other lake in the White Mountains. It's beautiful and, at 9000 feet, has a good stand of ponderosa pines and aspens on its southern shore that harbors all of its 250 campsites and facilities. Elk, deer, and turkey, along with the occasional bear, are common sights. Usually there's a pair of eagles somewhere close by to delight the birdwatchers.

Clair Spillman started the Big Lake Store and Marina in 1952 and it has been in her family ever since. Rick Law and his wife, Clotilda, are the current owners; they can be found working the store almost daily from early-spring ice-out until the snow is so deep that survival (and not fishing) becomes the priority. I call Rick often during the season to find out how the action is and can always rely on an accurate report. Rick is a real believer (and rightly so) in watching the weather fronts that pass through. He can usually predict to the day when the brook trout spawn will begin.

At 600 acres, Big Lake is appropriately named. The dam was raised in the early 1960s and the lake has not suffered a winterkill since. This also made the lake deeper than most in the area, so it doesn't suffer the weed problems associated with shallower lakes.

Big Lake maintained its water quality and fished better than any other lake through the summer of 1997. I caught many hard-fighting cutthroat, rainbow, and brook trout here that year. The strain of cutthroat in this lake is a particularly strong fighter; I have often been impressed with the fight these fish put up. Brookies, for some reason, didn't come on as strong in 1997 as in previous years. There is always a good population of rainbows

RON DUNGAN

Crescent Lake

here; more than 30,000 are planted each spring and fall. The fish grow big and fast in Big Lake. The records for 1997 were a 6½-pound rainbow, a 6½-pound cutthroat, and a 3-pound brook trout.

Fish the lake in early spring with Big buggers that resemble crawdads. A lot of anglers use Peacock Ladies, Warden's Worries, and a fly invented by local tier, Will Amerson, called the Crystal Flash. Early-season March browns can give you some top-water action, but are usually sporadic. Fish the edges early, when the big trout are cruising the warmer, shallow water for crawdads or fathead minnows that made it through the winter. I have had some great early-season fishing on Big Lake for cruising brookies and rainbows. As the season progresses, I switch to a faster-sinking line and get my fly deeper in the water column. The lake has a few weeds in the backs of some of its coves, where you can find some mayfly activity. This is not a great damselfly lake, but I have done well with small *Baetis* patterns on calmer evenings in the backs of the weedier coves. When all else fails, I use the old "Big Lake fishing logic"—put on something with a red tail. More times than not, this seems to be the ticket.

Big Lake can be reached by heading east on AZ 273 past Sunrise Lake to Forest Road 113; driving south from Eagar on AZ 261; or, from the east, taking Forest Road 249 off US 180/191. You can give Rick Law a call for the weather forecast and current fishing conditions at (520) 521-1387.

CRESCENT LAKE

Rating: 7
Access: Good
Seasons: Year-round
Maps: DeLorme p. 53, White Mountain Apache maps
Positives: Rich lake, grows fish fast; good damsel hatch; boat rental; store and marina
Negatives: Suffers periodic winterkills, gets weedy in summer, can be windy

Crescent is just up the road from Big Lake, and its store and marina are also owned by the Law family. Still, although these two lakes are very close, they're vastly different and fish differently, also. Crescent is quite a bit smaller—130 to 150 acres when full—and much shallower than Big Lake. It's a richer lake and grows large fish even faster than Big Lake. It's characterized by large patches of weeds, which can become a real problem to the float tuber, although they also serve as insect factories and give the flourishing population of damsels and fathead minnows here some protection from the marauding brookies and rainbows. I love to fish weedy lakes, because I know somewhat where the trout "should" be. Fish the edges and cast into the pockets—that's where the bigger trout will be. They find security, protection from predators, and food all in the same place. When the bigger fish are locked into the cover, it often pays to abandon dredging with your sinking line and put on a floater. Cast into the pockets and seams with a nymph and let it sink down the edges of the weeds. Work the fly *slowly* with short, erratic strips or a figure-8 hand retrieve. Bigger fish hide in these pockets, especially when the sun is high in the sky. A floating line will land more softly on the water, and you won't be dragging your fly through the weeds. Your main problem will be getting the nice fish you hook out of the weeds—always a nice problem to have!

Crescent has one of the better damselfly hatches on the mountain, and the rainbows and brookies feed heavily on these insects when the hatch begins, usually in June or early July. Crescent has good *Callibaetis* and *Baetis* populations as well. Hare's Ears and Pheasant Tails work well throughout the season, as do buggers and leeches. Try size 14s early, and go smaller as the season progresses. Midges are prolific on Crescent and the trout are always willing to take advantage of this hatch, which comes off daily on schedule if weather conditions remain stable. I have always been amazed at how much trout depend on such tiny morsels for a food source. Most of the midges that come off on our lakes are size 20 or smaller, and it must take an awful lot of feeding on them to satisfy a trout's appetite. But they consume the midges on a daily basis, sometimes to the point of ignoring larger food sources.

I was fishing Crescent with my buddies Don Carlson, Doug Esquivel, and Jack Morales one day in early July. A good damsel hatch was coming off and we were picking up a lot of nice rainbows and brookies on damsel nymphs. All at the same time, we stopped catching fish. When I looked around, I noticed a good hatch of midges emerging. So I switched to a midge pattern just trailed off my damsel nymph and immediately started catching fish again. This lasted for about 20 minutes, and then the trout switched back to feeding on the damsel hatch again. Which all goes to show how dependent the trout become on the daily midge hatch. They'll suspend all other feeding activities to indulge at this daily smorgasbord . . . even if it means taking 200 midges to make up the same nutrient total as one damsel nymph.

Crescent can be reached from the same access roads as Big Lake. For lake conditions, call Rick Law at Big Lake.

GREER LAKES

Rating: 7
Access: Good
Seasons: Year-round
Maps: DeLorme p. 53, White Mountain Apache map
Positives: Big brown trout; campgrounds, general store, and boat
   rentals nearby; paved road
Negatives: Fishing slows in summer

The Greer Lakes—Tunnel, Bunch, and River Reservoirs—are within walking distance of one another, located about a mile from the town of Greer. They're usually the first lakes I hit in spring; At 8200 feet, they're the first to come out of winter's grip and provide good early-season action for browns and rainbows. Call Will and Phyllis Amerson at the Circle B Market (which they manage for owner Mark Jones) to find out how soon you can get on the water. They're always at the store—unless Will is off fishing somewhere—and can tell you what the action is like on any of the lakes throughout the season. Will is also one of the state's best innovative tiers and can always help you out with fly selection. The phone number of the Circle B Market is (520) 735-7540.

Tunnel Reservoir

A small lake of 44 acres, Tunnel is the more consistently productive of the three. It's shallow and rather bowl-like, so wading is effective, especially in early spring when the trout are cruising the shorelines looking for crawdads. Tunnel has lots of rainbows, and some large browns come out of it every season, too. Phyllis told me about a brown of almost 5 pounds that was recently taken when most nearby lakes hadn't thawed yet.

Early in the season I fish predominantly brown buggers in this lake. The trout have been feeding on the crawdads under the ice, and a brown Sparkle Bugger imitates them well. During the summer months, Elk Hair Caddis and mayfly imitations work on rainbows and browns, especially at dusk. The lake can come alive with feeding trout—you can take a fish on every cast.

Bunch Reservoir

Bunch is just across the road from Tunnel and is about the same size, with many of the same characteristics. Although both are rather shallow, they never stay frozen long enough to winterkill. Bunch has a good population of big browns but doesn't get as much fishing pressure as the other two Greer Lakes, so it gives you the best chance of the three for that wall-mount.

River Reservoir

River is the largest Greer Lake and sees more fishing pressure than either of the other two. It spreads 120 acres when full and holds a good population of big browns and rainbows. This lake is deeper, especially at the dam end, and can be hard to fly-fish at times. It fishes well in spring and fall, but trout go deep in the summer months, becoming harder to catch. River doesn't have many weeds, so patterns that imitate small baitfish and crawdads work well, as in all three Greer Lakes. Terry Chartier, a long-time fishing friend, has done well here in early spring using *Chironomid* on a floating line. He uses a dry-fly line with a long leader and fine tippet, and slowly hand-twists his midge off the bottom. He has had some excellent days with this method. I use this technique often when the heat of summer has driven the fish into deeper, cooler water. When the trout seem to ignore all your best offerings, try a tiny midge. Sometimes it'll be enough to get even the toughest closed-mouth trout to play.

The lakes can be reached if you're coming east from Pinetop or south from Springerville by taking AZ 373 east off AZ 260.

MOGOLLON RIM LAKES

The Rim lakes consist of seven impoundments on the Mogollon Rim in central Arizona—Woods Canyon, Willow Springs, Chevelon Canyon, Bear Canyon, Knoll, Blue Ridge, and Black Canyon. Except for Black Canyon all of these are similar in structure; they were all formed by the damming of streams in deep canyons. They're deep and, for the most part, have few weeds. All have crawdads, which the trout key on as a major food source. I'll look at several of these lakes. *To reach the S end of Chevelon (harder to get to) take FR 300 Woods Canyon and continue 8 miles until FR 169 and go 7.6 miles. R on FR 119 to FR 180 and turn L which will end after 4 miles. Look for hand written sign that says — ends .5 miles. Park and hike down*

CHEVELON CANYON LAKE

Rating: 6
Access: Fair
Seasons: Sp, F
Maps: DeLorme p. 51, Sitgreaves National forest maps
Positives: Big brown trout, easy to find solitude, abundant wildlife
Negatives: Long hike in and out, hard to fish in summer

Chevelon Canyon Lake is a good early-spring and late-fall fishery. It holds plenty of big browns, and good rainbows as well. It's one of the few lakes on which the state has placed some special regulations—it's managed as a lure-and-fly-only lake, with a slot limit of 10 to 14 inches. All fish in this size range must be returned to the lake unharmed; officials have determined that these trout are the prime breeders.

This is not the lake for the portly couch potato to fish. It's long and narrow, and accessed at either end by a long, steep trail down and back up. I swear the climb back up is twice as long as the climb down. I usually fish the southern end of the lake, where Chevelon Creek flows in. This creek is formed at the confluence of the streams coming from Woods Canyon and Willow Springs. It flows high and off-color in spring (from the runoff) and has a good run of rainbows, which go upstream some distance to spawn. I've also caught some nice browns that were following the rainbows upstream to chow down on their eggs. Depending on the severity of the winter and how early spring comes to the high country, you can get into Chevelon Canyon Lake by April—sometimes. The forest service closes the roads until the threat of winter storms is over to prevent foolhardy fishermen from getting stuck in the inevitable quagmire of spring.

I use big buggers in the spring in Chevelon Canyon Lake—usually brown, but that's just my choice. The trout feed heavily on crawdads throughout winter, and brown imitates them well. Chevelon Canyon Lake

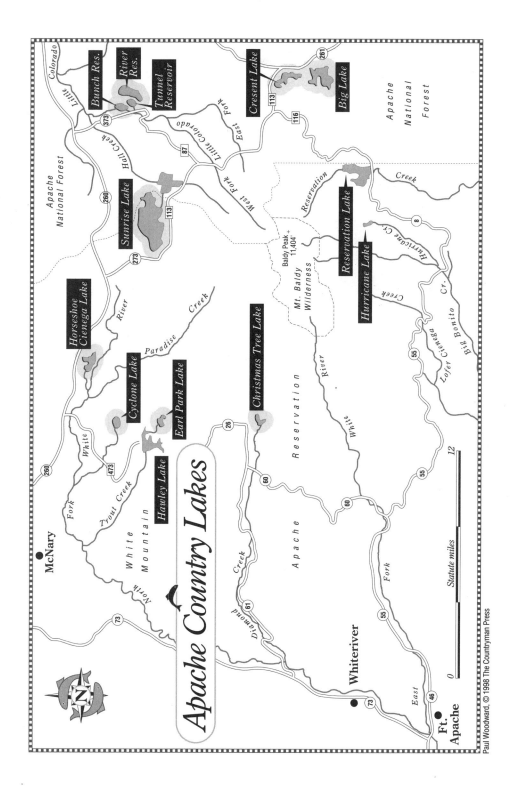

Apache Country Lakes

Bunch Res.

River Res.

Tunnel Reservoir

Cresent Lake

Big Lake

Sunrise Lake

Horseshoe Cienega Lake

Cyclone Lake

Earl Park Lake

Christmas Tree Lake

Hawley Lake

Reservation Lake

Hurricane Lake

Apache National Forest

Apache National Forest

Apache National Forest

Reservation

Apache Reservation

Mt. Baldy Wilderness

Baldy Peak
11,404'

Colorado

Little

Little Colorado

East Fork

West Fork

Hall Creek

Paradise Creek

White River

White Mountain

Trout Creek

North Fork

White Fork

Diamond Creek

East Fork

Reservation Creek

White River

Hurricane Cr.

Lofer Cienega

Big Bonito

Creek

McNary

Whiteriver

Ft. Apache

Statute miles

0   12

N

373

260

273

113

87

261

113

116

26

60

60

55

55

55

55

8

473

260

73

61

46

73

Paul Woodward, © 1998 The Countryman Press

RON DUNGAN

Willow Springs Lake

is at 6400 feet and will freeze over in winter, but regularly opens during extended periods of warm weather. Access during this time is by snowmobile, so the lake doesn't get much pressure and—more importantly—has no chance of winterkill. This is what allows this lake to grow large fish, because it's not bug rich and the trout have to depend mostly on leeches, crawdads, and smaller baitfish to survive the winter. I've caught some snakelike browns at ice-out after severe winters. After summer warms the water though, things become a little easier for the trout. The season's newly hatched trout fry become fair game for the resident holdovers, and little crawdads can be found in the shallows. I like to get on the water in early morning and cast from the shoreline; I use a brown Sparkle Bugger with bead-chain eyes and a pair of rubber legs. The browns will come up onto shallow shoals during the night, feeding opportunistically on crawdads and small baitfish. After the sun hits the water, they drop back down into the deeper channels and usually have to be dredged for with sinking lines from a float tube.

I've hit some caddis hatches on this lake, but the best top-water fishing I've seen here is during the cicada hatch. This insect looks much like a large, winged beetle. Quite a few different varieties inhabit Arizona, from the timbered country down to the desert. These bugs live underground feeding on tree roots for as long as 17 years before they emerge from the ground, climb up the tree, and shed their skin to become a winged adult that looks much like a big stonefly only uglier. When cicadas emerge—usually from May to August, depending on the species—trout go crazy for them. They're fun to fish, too, because you present your imitation much as you would a hopper pattern: Slap the fly down hard on the water to draw the trout's attention. The take will be anything but dainty. The cicadas are big enough to draw the attention of even the largest trout in the lake. I've caught fish after the hatch has been going for a while and their stomachs feel like they've been eating marbles.

If you're feeling frisky and don't mind a hike, Chevelon Canyon Lake is a good bet. I'm not getting any younger myself; and every time I hit this lake, I swear it's going to be the last time. But when spring comes around or the threat of the first winter storm is in the air, Chevelon is always on my mind. It's a great lake to fish during those times: It brings to mind cold and wind and big fish.

Chevelon Canyon Lake is in the Sitgreaves National Forest about 60 miles from Payson. It can be reached by taking AZ 260 east to Forest Road (FR) 300. Take FR 300 to FR 169, and turn north onto FR 169. To access the southern end of the lake, take FR 169 to FR 119, then FR 119 to FR 180. Follow FR 180 to the primitive campgrounds at the end of the lake. To access the northern end of the lake (where you'll find the dam and good camping facilities), take FR 169 past FR 119 and turn off onto FR 169B.

WOODS CANYON LAKE AND
WILLOW SPRINGS LAKE

Rating: 6
Access: Good
Seasons: Year-round
Maps: DeLorme p. 51, Sitgreaves National Forest maps
Positives: General store, boat rentals, campgrounds, lots of stocked trout
Negatives: Crowded, angling pressure

I've grouped these two lakes together because they're so close to each another and so similar in their fishing. Both have campgrounds and boat rentals. Both receive a fresh supply of catchable rainbows weekly during summer. Both lakes are accessed by paved road, and together they're the two most heavily fished lakes on the Rim. These lakes are frequented mostly by families wanting to beat the valley heat and get away to the mountains for a few days. Many kids in the Valley of the Sun caught their first rainbow trout on these lakes. I try not to hit them at the peak of summer vacation, because of the crowds and abundance of stocked trout. But hit either of these lakes in early spring before the stocking begins and you

Woods Canyon Lake

can catch some nice rainbows cruising the shorelines. The same can be said of fall, when everyone has put the fly-rods away and gotten out shotguns or deer rifles (or schoolbooks), and the big browns are thinking about reproduction. Hit the gravelly shorelines or spots where enough current enters or exits the lake to make the trout think they can spawn and you can experience some great action.

Several years ago these lakes had a very mild winter. The ice on Willow Springs kept opening and closing all season, and after every warm spell little runoff streams would enter the lake. I talked to a lot of anglers who told me of brook trout running up these little runoff stream to spawn. So even these easy-to-reach lakes can yield very large trout if you're here at the right time.

Woods Canyon and Willow Springs hold wary browns and don't winterkill, so there will always be big fish to catch here—just don't go during summer vacation. These lakes can be reached by taking AZ 260 east from Payson. Woods Canyon is off Forest Road (FR) 300, and Willow Springs is 1 mile east of the Woods Canyon turnoff, on FR 149.

BLUE RIDGE RESERVOIR

Rating: 6
Access: Good
Seasons: Year-round
Maps: DeLorme p. 43, Coconino National Forest maps
Positives: Big trout; little fishing pressure, campgrounds
Negatives: Managed for native fish, deep lake is hard to fly-fish

I think Blue Ridge Lake is the sleeper fishery on the Rim, if not in the entire state. For the past three years, the Arizona Game and Fish Department has not stocked this lake much; it has been managed as a native fish lake. This means limited transplants of exotic game fish, namely rainbow and brown trout. At first glance you might think this a loss to Arizona's fishermen. However, Blue Ridge has a year-round stream feeding into it—East Clear Creek, from the north. Browns and rainbows migrate up this stream from the lake each fall and spring to spawn. Recent nettings by the Game and Fish Department found large numbers of big trout, rainbows and browns, in the lake. This could be your best chance to catch the trout of a lifetime.

Blue Ridge is much like the other Rim lakes—deep and with an abundance of crawdads. Fishing large streamers and big buggers will entice some of the large trout to play. Fishing extra-fast-sinking lines is the ticket here, unless the cicadas are buzzing in the trees. This lake can get a good hatch of cicadas anytime from early spring to the end of summer. Make sure you bring a floating line with you, and any big bushy fly that floats. When the cicada hatch starts you won't see technical fishing. In fact, this hatch reminds me of the beginning of Montana's salmonfly hatch—you wonder why these fish are taking your fly when they already have so many cicadas already in their stomachs!

To get to Blue Ridge, take Forest Road 751 off AZ 87 out of Strawberry.

10

Patterns for Arizona
Rivers and Streams

I'll never forget the first time I planned to fly-fish the great trout waters of the West, more than 30 years ago. I called a well-known writer in Montana and asked him what kind of hatches I could expect. And I'll never forget his reply.

"You won't see any hatches on most streams and lakes in the West. A few of them hold some stoneflies—other than that you won't see much," that famous writer explained.

How wrong he proved to be.

I've heard similar descriptions of southwestern waters—including Arizona's. Several anglers I spoke to said that few hatches appear in Arizona. And in part they are correct: Lack of precipitation is one of Arizona's biggest downfalls. If the Mogollon Rim and the White Mountains receive less-than-normal snowfall, trout streams certainly suffer—and so do hatches.

In chapter 2 I indicated that you'll find plenty of little blue-winged olives, blue quills, and little black stoneflies on Arizona trout streams. And you will, but you may also experience times without hatches. So I've divided this chapter into two sections, the first on patterns that match the hatches and patterns that consistently work when there are no hatches, the second on patterns that match Arizona's most common hatches. You'll note that I've included patterns for nymphs, emergers, duns, and spinners.

HOOKS

For years I used only Mustad hooks, but about five years ago I switched to Daiichi hooks for my Trico patterns. I've had so much success with them that I now use Daiichi hooks for many patterns. For dry patterns that copy duns, spinners, and emergers I suggest a Daiichi 1190 (barbless), 1180 (minibarb), or 1170 (standard dry-fly hook). The only difference I see among these three dry-fly hooks is the barb. To copy nymphs I recommend a Daiichi 1710.

I use a Daiichi 1310 in size 20 to tie my Trico patterns. It's a short-shanked dry-fly hook, using it in a size 20 will give you much more successful hooking action than would the standard size 24. For emerging caddis pupae try a Daiichi 1130. For patterns like the Muddler and Peacock Lady, try a Daiichi 2220.

PATTERNS WHEN NO HATCH APPEARS

Beadhead patterns have evolved into important wet flies in the past decade. They work extremely well on Arizona lakes, rivers, and streams. The Olive Beadhead, Tan Beadhead, Beadhead Pheasant Tail, and Green Weenie have all proved to be great patterns when no hatch appears. And don't be without the Patriot, an attractor dry-fly pattern that works consistently in a wide variety of fishing situations.

THE PATRIOT
Hook: Sizes 12 to 18
Thread: Red
Tail: Brown hackle fibers
Body: Smolt blue Krystal Flash wound around the shank. Wind some of the red thread in the middle of the shank, similar to the Royal Coachman.
Wings: White impala or calf tail, divided
Hackle: Brown

GREEN WEENIE
Hook: Sizes 10 to 12
Body: Cut off a 4- or 5-inch piece of chartreuse chenille. Tie the piece in at the bend of the hook and form a small loop with the chenille that extends out over the bend by about an inch. Then wrap the remainder of the chenille around the bend of the hook up to the eye.

CHARLES MECK

Beadhead Pheasant Tail Nymph

BEADHEAD PHEASANT TAIL NYMPH
Hook: Sizes 12 to 20
Thread: Dark brown
Tail: Five fibers from a ringneck pheasant tail
Body: Continue winding the pheasant tail fibers used for the tail up to the bead, tie in, and cut off the butt section
Hackle: About 10 to 15 pheasant tail fiber tips spread around the eye of the hook
Thorax: Copper bead

DARK OLIVE BEADHEAD
Hook: Sizes 12 to 20
Thread: Dark Olive
Body: Dark olive angora, dubbed, and ribbed with fine gold wire
Thorax: Copper bead

TAN CADDIS BEADHEAD
Hook: Sizes 12 to 20
Thread: Tan
Body: Tan Squirrel Brite, dubbed
Thorax: Copper bead

STREAMERS FOR ARIZONA WATERS

I'll never forget the first day I fly-fished Sunrise Lake. While Craig Josephson, Bob David, and Josh David used Peacock Lady patterns, I used the infamous Green Weenie. In the first hour the three of them caught more than a dozen trout, while I caught none. I finally succumbed and tried a Peacock Lady. Within an hour I caught eight trout on that pattern.

There's another pattern that works especially well on Arizona streams and rivers. I fished the Little Colorado River at the X-Diamond Ranch several years ago during high water; late-March snowmelt had pushed the small river 2 feet above its normal level. Nothing I used seemed to work—until in a fit of frustration I tied on a Biggidy-Eyed Chook. (Preston Mauk of Altooona, Pennsylvania, first tied this particular streamer; if you ever meet Preston and ask him about the pattern, he'll immediately hand you one and ask you to try it.) The heavy fly sank to the bottom quickly and on my first cast I had a strike. In an hour of fishing that awkward pattern I caught a half-dozen trout. The pattern is difficult to cast but it really works, all across the United States, especially in heavy water.

PEACOCK LADY
Hook: Mustad 79580, size 10
Thread: Black
Body: Two or three strands of peacock wound up to the eye
Hackle: Wind a small grizzly hackle at the bend of the hook. The barbules of the hackle should be as long as the gap of the hook. Wind a brown hackle with barbules about twice as long as the grizzly hackle just behind the eye.
Tying Notes: Tie some of the Peacock Ladies with lead wire. If I plan to fish heavy water, I use 25 wraps of .015-inch wire. Also try a beadhead on some patterns. Both the weight and the beadhead will allow you to get deeper quicker.

BIGGIDY-EYED CHOOK
Hook: Size 4, 4X long
Thread: Black
Eye: Lead glass eyes
Tail: 10 strands of smolt blue Krystal Flash mixed with 30 strands black maribou
Body: Olive chenille, palmered with grizzly hackle

PATTERNS TO MATCH THE HATCHES

Order Ephemeroptera: Mayflies

BLUE QUILL
Copies all *Paraleptophlebia* species, including *debilis, heteronea, memorialis, gregalis,* and *bicornuta*
Hook: Size 18
Thread: Dark gray-brown
Tail: Medium gray hackle fibers
Body: Eyed peacock herl, stripped
Wings: Dark gray hackle tips
Hackle: Medium gray or dun

BLUE QUILL SPINNER
Hook: Size 18
Thread: Dark brown
Tail: Dark brown hackle fibers
Body: Dark brown poly, dubbed
Wings: Pale gray poly yarn, tied spent

PARA NYMPH
Hook: Sizes 16 and 18
Thread: Dark brown
Tail: Mallard flank feather, dyed dark brown
Body: Dark brown angora, dubbed
Wings: One dark gray mallard quill
Hackle: Dark gray

PARA EMERGER
Hook: Sizes 16 and 18
Thread: Dark brown
Tail: Dark brown hackle fibers
Body: Dark grayish brown angora, dubbed
Wing: Gray poly yarn pulled over top of dubbed brown angora
Hackle: Dark brown hackle fibers

BLUE DUN OR LITTLE BLUE-WINGED OLIVE DUN
Copies *Baetis bicaudatus, tricaudatus, intermedius,* and others
Hook: Sizes 18 and 20
Thread: Dark gray
Tail: Medium to dark gray hackle fibers
Body: Gray muskrat or medium gray poly with a slight olive cast, dubbed. (The body of *Baetis bicaudatus* is more olive than the others.)
Wings: On smaller sizes (20) use dark gray mallard quills; on larger sizes use dark gray hackle tips
Hackle: Blue dun

BLUE DUN II
Hook: Sizes 18, 20, and 22
Thread: Dark olive
Tail: None
Body: Fine medium olive vernille extending back ⅛ inch past the bend of the hook. Tie in body by ribbing.
Wings: Gray turkey
Hackle: Gray

RUSTY SPINNER
Hook: sizes 18 and 20
Thread: Dark brown
Tail: Dark grayish brown hackle fibers
Body: Grayish brown poly, dubbed and ribbed with fine tan thread

Wings: Pale gray poly yarn, tied spent

BAETIS NYMPH
Hook: Sizes 18 and 20
Thread: Dark olive
Tail: Wood duck fibers, dyed dark olive
Body: Dark olive brown opossum
Wings: Dark gray mallard quill section
Hackle: Cree, dyed dark olive

BAETIS EMERGER
Hook: Sizes 18 and 20
Thread: Dark olive
Tail: Wood duck fibers, dyed dark olive
Body: Dark olive-brown opossum
Wings: Dark gray mallard quill section

TRICO
Copies all *Tricorythodes* species
Hook: Sizes 20 to 24
Thread: Pale olive
Tail: Cream hackle fibers
Body: Pale olive poly, dubbed
Wings: Pale gray hackle tips
Hackle: Cream

TRICO SPINNER
Hook: Sizes 20 to 24
Thread: Dark brown
Tail: Female: short cream hackle fibers; male: long dark brown moose mane
Body: Female: rear third is cream poly, dubbed, and front two-thirds is dark brown dubbed poly; male: dark brown poly dubbed and ribbed with a fine light tan thread

Wings: White poly yarn, tied spent

TRICO NYMPH
Hook: Size 22
Thread: Black
Tail: Dark brown hackle fibers
Body: Dark brownish black fur
Wings: Dark gray mallard quill section
Hackle: Dark reddish brown

PALE EVENING DUN
Copies species like *Heptagenia elegantula*
Hook: Sizes 16 to 20
Thread: Pale yellow
Tail: Cream hackle fibers
Body: Pale yellowish cream poly, dubbed
Wings: Pale yellow hackle tips
Hackle: Cream

PALE EVENING SPINNER
Hook: Sizes 16 to 20
Thread: Cream
Tail: Cream hackle fibers
Body: Pale yellowish cream poly, dubbed
Wings: Pale gray poly yarn, tied spent

PALE EVENING NYMPH
Hook: Size 14
Thread: Dark brown
Tail: Mallard flank fibers, dyed brown
Body: Dark brown angora, loosely dubbed
Wings: Dark mallard section
Hackle: Grouse

PALE EVENING EMERGER
Hook: Size 14

Thread: Tan
Tail: Brown grouse
Body: Tan angora
Wings: Gray poly
Hackle: Grouse

PALE MORNING DUN
Copies species like *Ephemerella inermis, infrequens,* and *lacustris*
Hook: Sizes 16 and 18
Thread: Cream
Tail: Cream hackle fibers
Body: Varies from a bright olive to a creamish yellow. Use poly and dub.
Wings: Pale gray hackle tips
Hackle: Cream

PALE MORNING SPINNER
Hook: Sizes 16 and 18
Thread: Orange
Tail: Tan
Body: Tan
Wings: Pale gray poly yarn

PALE MORNING NYMPH
Hook: Size 16 or 18
Thread: Dark brown
Tail: Mallard flank fibers, dyed ginger
Body: Belly is amber angora or nymph dubbing with a darker brown back
Wings: Brown turkey
Hackle: Cree

PALE MORNING EMERGER
Hook: Size 16 or 18
Thread: Tan
Tail: Grouse
Body: Angora
Wings: White poly yarn

Hackle: Grouse
Tying note: Dun body colors vary tremendously from river to river

DARK RED QUILL
Copies species like *Cinygmula par*
Hook: Size 16
Thread: Brown
Tail: Medium dun hackle fibers
Body: Dark reddish brown hackle stem, stripped
Wings: Dark mallard quills, dark gray calf tail, or hackle tips
Hackle: Bronze dun

RED QUILL SPINNER
Hook: Size 16 or 18
Thread: Brown
Tail: Pale dun hackle fibers
Body: Reddish brown hackle stem
Wings: Pale tan poly, tied spent
Hackle: Brown

RED QUILL NYMPH
Hook: Size 16
Thread: Dark brown
Tail: Mallard flank, dyed amber
Body: Dark grayish brown Furry Foam over amber angora
Wings: Dark mallard quill
Hackle: Dark grouse or partridge

DARK RED QUILL EMERGER
Hook: Size 16
Thread: Brown
Tail: Light green
Body: Dark brown angora
Wings: Dark gray poly
Hackle: Brown grouse

QUILL GORDON
Copies western species like *Epeorus longimanus*

Hook: Size 14
Thread: Gray
Tail: Medium dun hackle
Body: Pale to medium gray poly or muskrat fur, dubbed
Wings: Dark mallard quills, dark gray calf tail, or dark gray hackle tips
Hackle: Pale tannish gray

QUILL GORDON NYMPH
Hook: Size 14
Thread: Dark brown
Tail: Mallard flank, dyed amber
Body: Dark brown Furry Foam over the top
Wings: Dark mallard quill
Hackle: Dark grouse or partridge

QUILL GORDON EMERGER
Hook: Size 14
Thread: Brown
Tail: Medium grayish brown angora
Body: Dark gray poly yarn
Wings: Brown grouse

RED QUILL SPINNER
Hook: Size 14
Thread: Tan
Tail: Moose mane
Body: Pale yellowish brown poly
Wings: Pale tan poly
Hackle: Ginger with a turn of brown

SPECKLE-WINGED DUN
Copies *Callibaetis americanus* and other closely related species
Hook: Size 14 and 16
Thread: Tan
Tail: Cream-ginger hackle fibers
Body: Medium gray poly

Wings: Dark gray mallard flank
Hackle: Pale bronze dun

SPECKLE-WINGED SPINNER
Hook: Sizes 14 and 16
Thread: Gray
Tail: Cream-ginger hackle fibers
Body: Pale gray poly
Wings: Mallard flank feather
Hackle: Pale bronze dun

SPECKLE-WINGED NYMPH
Hook: Size 14
Thread: Brown
Tail: Pheasant tail fibers
Body: Medium brown angora
Wings: Dark mallard quill
Hackle: Dark brown grouse

SPECKLE-WINGED EMERGER
Hook: Size 14
Thread: Brown
Tail: Dark grouse
Body: Tannish gray angora
Wings: Gray turkey
Hackle: Dark grouse

WESTERN GREEN DRAKE
Copies species like *Drunella grandis*
Hook: Size 10 or 12
Thread: Dark olive
Tail: Moose mane
Body: Olive-black poly, ribbed with pale yellow thread
Wings: Impala, dyed dark gray
Hackle: Grayish black

GREAT RED SPINNER
Hook: Size 10 or 12
Thread: Black
Tail: Moose mane
Body: Olive-black poly, ribbed with pale yellow thread

Wings: White poly, tied spent
Hackle: Brownish black

Green Drake Nymph
Hook: Size 12
Thread: Dark brown
Tail: Amber mallard flank feather
Body: Dark olive angora
Wings: Mottled brown turkey
Hackle: Olive-brown

Light Cahill
Copies species like *Cinygma dimicki*
Hook: Size 12
Thread: Yellow
Tail: Ginger hackle fibers
Body: Pale creamish yellow poly
Wings: Wood duck (or imitation) flank feather
Hackle: Ginger-cream

Light Cahill Spinner
Hook: Size 12
Thread: Yellow
Tail: Ginger hackle fibers
Body: Yellowish cream poly
Wings: Pale gray poly
Hackle: Yellowish cream

Pale Brown Dun
Copies species like *Cinygmula reticulata*
Hook: Size 12 or 14
Thread: Tan
Tail: Ginger-cream hackle fibers
Body: Pale brown poly
Wings: Yellow mallard flank
Hackle: Ginger-cream

Dark Rusty Spinner
Hook: Size 12 or 14
Thread: Brown

Tail: Dark brown hackle fibers
Body: Dark brown poly
Wings: Pale yellow poly
Hackle: Dark brown

Pink Lady
Copies species like *Epeorus albertae*
Hook: Size 12
Thread: Cream
Tail: Cream-ginger hackle fibers
Body: Grayish cream poly
Wings: Gray mallard quills or dark gray hackle tips
Hackle: Cream or badger

Salmon Spinner
Hook: Size 12
Thread: Cream
Tail: Dark brown moose mane
Body: Female: pinkish red poly; male: cream-gray poly
Wings: Pale gray poly
Hackle: Pale blue dun

Pink Lady Nymph
Hook: Size 12
Thread: Brown
Tail: Brown mallard flank
Body: Medium brown Furry Foam over tan angora
Wings: Light mottled turkey
Hackle: Sandy dun

Pink Lady Emerger
Hook: Size 12
Thread: Brown
Tail: Brown grouse
Body: Tan poly yarn
Wings: Light grouse

GRAY FOX

Copies many species like *Heptagenia solitaria*
Hook: Size 12
Thread: Tan
Tail: Bronze dun hackle fibers
Body: Yellowish tan poly
Wings: Pale gray hackle tips
Hackle: Bronze dun

GINGER QUILL SPINNER

Hook: Size 12
Thread: Tan
Tail: Ginger hackle fibers
Body: Eyed peacock herl, dyed tan and stripped
Wings: Pale gray poly
Hackle: Ginger

GRAY FOX NYMPH

Hook: Size 14
Thread: Brown
Tail: Brown mallard flank
Body: Dark brown over pale yellow Furry Foam
Wings: Dark mottled turkey
Hackle: Grouse or partridge

GRAY FOX EMERGER

Hook: Size 14
Thread: Tan
Tail: Brown grouse
Body: Tan angora
Wings: Brown poly
Hackle: Brown grouse

PALE BROWN DUN

Copies *Rhithrogena hageni*
Hook: Size 12
Thread: Olive
Tail: Cream hackle fibers
Body: Tannish olive poly
Wings: Gray mallard quills or dark gray hackle tips
Hackle: Cream-ginger

PALE BROWN NYMPH

Hook: Size 12
Thread: Dark brown
Tail: A few wood duck fibers
Body: Greenish brown rabbit with claret hackle
Wings: Dark brown turkey
Hackle: Dark brown

PALE BROWN DUN EMERGER

Hook: Size 12
Thread: Tan
Tail: Light grouse
Body: Light grayish olive angora
Wings: Brown poly yarn
Hackle: Brown grouse

DARK TAN SPINNER

Hook: Size 12
Thread: Tan
Tail: Gray hackle fibers
Body: Pale olive-tan poly
Wings: Pale gray poly
Hackle: Cream mixed with dark tan

DARK BROWN DUN

Copies species like *Ameletus velox*
Hook: Size 12 or 14
Thread: Dark brown
Tail: Dark brown hackle fibers
Body: Dark brown poly
Wings: Teal flank feather
Hackle: Dark brown

DARK BROWN SPINNER

Hook: Size 12 or 14
Thread: Dark brown
Tail: Dark brown hackle fibers
Body: Dark brown poly
Wings: Teal flank feather, dyed yellow

Hackle: Dark brown

BLACK QUILL
Copies *Choroterpes* spp.
Hook: Size 14
Thread: Dark brown
Tail: Dark bronze dun hackle fibers
Body: Eyed peacock herl, stripped
Wings: Dark gray hackle tips
Hackle: Dark brown hackle with a turn or two of tan hackle in the rear

EARLY BROWN SPINNER
Hook: Size 14
Thread: Dark brown
Tail: Dark brown hackle fibers
Body: Dark reddish brown poly ribbed with pale yellow thread
Wing: Pale tan poly
Hackle: Dark brown hackle

BLACK QUILL NYMPH
Hook: Size 12 or 14
Thread: Dark brown
Tail: Dark brown hackle fibers
Body: Chocolate brown angora, loosely dubbed
Wings: Dark mallard section
Hackle: Dark brown hackle

BLACK QUILL EMERGER
Hook: Size 14
Thread: Dark brown
Tail: Dark brown hackle fibers
Body: Dark brown rabbit
Wings: Dark gray poly yarn
Hackle: Dark grouse

BLUE DUN
Copies species like *Thraulodes bicornuta*
Hook: Size 14

Thread: Dark gray-brown
Tail: Medium gray hackle fibers
Body: Dark gray poly
Wings: Dark gray hackle tips
Hackle: Medium gray or dun

BLUE DUN SPINNER
Hook: Size 14
Thread: Dark brown
Tail: Dark brown hackle fibers
Body: Dark brown poly, dubbed
Wings: Pale gray poly yarn, tied spent

Order *Trichoptera*: Caddisflies

GREEN CADDIS
Copies some species in genera *Rhyacophila* and *Cheumatopsyche*
Hook: Sizes 14 and 16
Thread: Green
Body: Green poly
Wings: Brown deer body hair
Hackle: Tan. (Optional—deer hair.)

LITTLE BLACK CADDIS
Copies some species in genus *Chimarra*
Hook: Size 16
Thread: Black
Tail: Optional—add tan Z-Lon shuck
Body: Black poly, dubbed. Optional—wind a dark brown hackle in at the bend of the hook and palmer it to the eye. Clip off the barbules on top.
Wings: Dark brown deer or elk hair
Hackle: Optional—dark brown

TAN CADDIS

Copies many specie in the genus
Hydropsyche

Hook: Size 14 or 16
Thread: Tan
Body: Tan poly, dubbed
Wings: Light brown deer hair
Hackle: Tan

GRANNOM

Copies many species in genus
Brachycentrus

Hook: Sizes 12 to 16
Thread: Black or green, depending
on the body color you use
Body: Black or green poly, dubbed
Wings: Dark deer body hair, tied
downwing-style
Hackle: Optional—dark brown

Order *Plecoptera*: Stoneflies

LITTLE YELLOW STONEFLY

Copies species like *Skwala
parallela*

Hook: Size 16
Thread: Yellow
Tail: Short cream hackle fibers
Body: Pale yellow poly, dubbed
Wings: Cream hackle tips, tied
downwing-style
Hackle: Cree hackle

LITTLE YELLOW STONEFLY NYMPH

Hook: Size 16
Thread: Pale yellow
Tail: Pale yellow hackle fibers
Body: Pale yellow angora
Wings: Pale yellow mallard flank
Hackle: Pale yellow hackle

LITTLE BLACK STONEFLY

Copies species like *Encopnopsis
brevicanda*

Hook: Size 16
Thread: Black
Tail: Short black hackle fibers
Body: Black poly, dubbed
Wings: Pale gray deer hair

LITTLE BROWN STONEFLY

Copies some species in genus
Amphinemura

Hook: Sizes 16 and 18
Thread: Dark brown
Tail: Dark brown moose mane,
very short
Body: Dark brown poly
Wings: Gray deer hair

Order Diptera: *Chironomids* or midges

BLACK MIDGE PUPA

Hook: Sizes 18 to 24
Thread: Black
Body: Black Antron
Ribbing: Fine copper wire. Wing
case of white poly or Z-Lon
tied in lie short spinner wings.
Thorax: Black angora, dubbed
Tying Notes: Tie in the white poly
and make it extend ⅛ to ¼ inch
to the right and left of the
shank. Dub a liberal amount of
black angora behind and over
the top of the wing case. After
finishing the body and applying
the ribbing, tie in a piece of
white Z-Lon just behind the eye
of the hook. Dub the thorax
with muskrat, then bring the
piece of Z-Lon over top of the

thorax and tie in at the eye. Let the Z-Lon extend over the eye and ⅛ inch beyond.

STILLBORN MIDGE
Hook: Size 20
Thread: Black
Body: Black tying thread ribbed with fine copper wire. White Z-Lon tied on top and extending over the back and front.
Thorax: Black angora, dubbed
Tying Notes: Tie in the Z-Lon at the bend of the hook. Let a piece as long as the hook shank extend back over the hook. Pull the Z-Lon over the top of the completed body and secure with the ribbed copper wire. Let the Z-Lon extend out over the eye of the hook about ½ inch.

GRIFFITH'S GNAT
Hook: Sizes 20 to 26
Thread: Black
Body: Peacock herl
Hackle: Grizzly

11

Patterns for Arizona Lakes

Some of the insects found in Arizona's streams inhabit its lakes as well; the patterns to imitate these bugs described in chapter 10 work fine in the lakes. But many of the lake patterns I use are bigger than the insects found in streams. Flies that imitate leeches, big predatory dragonflies, and the diminutive damselfly work better in lakes than streams, because these insects are more often found in stillwater than the faster-moving currents of mountain streams. And although crayfish sometimes inhabit moving water, they're much more prevalent in Arizona's stillwaters, both high-mountain and lower-desert lakes. The crayfish is a hardy, versatile food source for all of Arizona's game fish.

This chapter is devoted to the patterns I use on the lakes. Some are generic patterns that your grandpa probably told you about; they've been used all over the world. Others are unique to Arizona—some new, some old. They all work here as well as every other piece of water on which I've tried them.

Dry flies, of course, were covered thoroughly in chapter 10. The patterns here are all subsurface and can be fished with floating, intermediate, sinking-tip, and full-sinking lines. The main criterion of your choice is to get the fly to the fish—the perfect pattern won't catch any fish if they can't see it! The second most important factor in successful lake fishing is presentation. When the fish aren't cooperating the way I'd like them to, it's usually my presentation that's wrong—not my pattern. Lakes fish differently. Different species of trout react differently to certain retrieves. Some require fast retrieves, others need painstakingly slow hand-twist retrieves. Up-and-down motion with short intermittent jerks works well on others.

183

Before you switch from a pattern the fish are refusing, try a different action. How many times have you been stripping your fly in patiently only to have a trout hit it the moment you lifted it to start your next cast? That trout was following your fly the whole time; the instant it made an upward motion—(much like an emerging insect)—the trout's instinct took over.

Leeches

All these patterns can be weighted on the front half of the hook with lead, weighted eyes, or beadheads.

WOOLLY BUGGER

Hook: Sizes 2 to 10, 2X to 3X long
Thread: Color to match body; 6/0 or 3/0
Tail: Marabou with several strands of Krystal Flash
Hackle: Saddle
Body: Chenille (usually brown, black, or olive)

SPARKLE BUGGER

Hook: Sizes 2 to 8, 2X to 3X long
Thread: 3/0
Tail: Marabou
Body: Teased Arizona Sparkle Yarn

DIAMOND BUGGER

Hook: Sizes 6 to 10, 2X to 3X long
Thread: 6/0 to 3/0
Tail: Marabou; match body
Hackle: Saddle
Body: Arizona Diamond Braid

SIMI SEAL LEECH

Hook: Sizes 4 to 8, 2X to 3X long
Thread: 3/0
Tail: Arizona Simi Seal, assorted colors

Rib: Wire
Body: Teased Arizona Simi Seal

JANSSEN LEECH

Hook: Sizes 4o to 12, 2X to 3X long
Thread: 3/0
Tail: Marabou, assorted colors
Body: Marabou

JR's GARBAGE LEECH

Hook: Sizes 10 to 14, 2X to 3X long
Thread: 6/0
Tail: Tips of three aftershaft feathers of ringneck pheasant
Rib: Fine gold or silver wire
Body: Three aftershaft feathers palmered up the hook shank
Try note: Sometimes I put a clear glass bead on the front

BUNNY LEECH

Hook: Sizes 2 to 6, 2X to 3X long
Thread: 3/0
Tail: Crosscut rabbit; optional—small clump of Krystal Flash
Body: Rabbit palmered up the hook shank

CAREY SPECIAL

Hook: Sizes 6 to 10, 2X to 4X long
Thread: Black, 6/0 or 3/0
Body: Arizona Synthetic Peacock, natural or bronze

Hackle: Lon pheasant rump feathers, tied wet-style

SIMULATOR
Hook: Sizes 6 to 12, 3X long
Thread: Brown, 6/0
Tail: Brown goose biots
Hackle: Brown saddle
Underwing: Arctic fox tail
Center: Arizona Diamond Hair
Body: Arizona Synthetic Peacock, natural
Rib: Fine gold or silver wire
Body: Three aftershaft feathers palmered up the hook shank

JR's UGLY BUG
Hook: Sizes 2 to 6
Thread: Color to match body; 3/0
Eyes: Dumbbell or bead chain
Tail: Sparse marabou tied the length of the hook shank
Body: Arizona Sparkle Yarn teased with Velcro
Legs: Two pairs of round rubber

GIRDLE BUG
Hook: Sizes 6 to 10, 2X to 3X long
Tail: Rubber tied in a V
Body: Chenille
Legs: Rubber

FOXY MINNOW
Hook: Mustad 3366, Sizes 4 to 12
Underwing: Arctic fox tail
Center: Arizona Diamond Hair
Overwing: Arctic fox tail

MATUKA
Hook: Sizes 4 to 8, 2X or 3X long
Rib: Copper, gold, or silver wire
Body: Arizona Sparkle Yarn or Arizona Diamond Braid

Wings: Soft webby hen hackle, dyed your color of choice
Hackle: Soft hen hackle

MUDDLER MINNOW
Hook: Sizes 2 to 10, 2X to 4X long
Thread: Tan monofilament, 3/0
Tail: Turkey fibers
Body: Flat gold tinsel
Underwing: Red squirrel tail or brown calf tail; optional—Krystal Flash
Wing: Paired sections of turkey wing
Collar: Deer hair tips
Head: Deer hair, trimmed to shape

CLOUSER CRAYFISH
Hook: Sizes 6 to 10, 3X long
Thread: 6/0
Antennae: Two bunches of ringneck pheasant tail, one short, one long
Nose (Tail): Natural hen mallard tail fibers
Back: Light mottled turkey quill or brown pheasant wing quill
Body: Pale gray yarn or dubbing
Claws: Natural hen mallard tail fibers
Rib: Gray thread, 6/0
Legs: Ginger, grizzly, or olive
Tying note: Can be tied in assorted colors

Damselflies and Dragonflies

JR's MARABOU DAMSEL (MATCH BODY COLOR)
Hook: Sizes 10 to 14, 2X long
Rib: Thread tag
Abdomen: 15 to 20 strands of

marabou, palmered two-thirds of the way up the hook shank

Wingcase: Pearl Saltwater Flashabou

Thorax: 15 to 20 strands of marabou, tied wet-fly style. At the head of the fly split the fibers evenly on both sides of the hook, tie down, and size by pinching between your fingers to attain the correct length.

JR's RABBIT DAMSEL

Hook: Sizes 10 to 12, 2X to 3X long

Thread: 6/0

Tail: Small clump of Arizona Rabbit Sheen or Arizona Crystal Rabbit

Rib: Thread tag

Abdomen: Thinly dubbed Arizona Rabbit Sheen or Arizona Crystal Rabbit two-thirds of the way up the hook shank

Wingcase: Turkey breast feather coated with Flexament or Scudback

Thorax: Arizona Rabbit Sheen or Arizona Crystal Rabbit dubbed twice as thick as abdomen and teased out to imitate legs

JANSSEN DAMSEL

Hook: Sizes 8 to 12, 2X to 3X long

Thread: 6/0

Tail: Small tuft of marabou

Rib: Thread tag

Abdomen: Thinly dubbed body material of choice two-thirds of the way up the hook shank

Wingcase: Turkey coated with epoxy

Hackle: Brown saddle clipped short to imitate legs

Thorax: Light olive chenille

HANGOVER

This is a great damsel pattern from Phil Therrien of Bishop, California

Hook: Tiemco 3761BL, size 1

Thread: Olive, 8/0

Tail: Olive Ozark mottled marabou

Eyes: Small green glass beads on 25-pound Amnesia, tied on the underside of the hook

Rib: Olive or clear Cascade V-Rib

Thorax: Arizona Synthetic Peacock, natural

Wingcase: Olive turkey quill

Legs: Olive grizzly rooster saddle hackle

WHITLOCK DAMSEL

Hook: Sizes 8 to 12, 2X to 3X long

Thread: Color to match body, 6/0

Eyes: Monofilament

Tail: Marabou

Rib: Gold oval tinsel

Abdomen: Antron (color to suit)

Legs: Mottled hen hackle

Thorax: Antron (same color as abdomen)

BARR'S DAMSEL

Hook: Tiemco 200R, sizes 8 to 12

Thread: Olive, 6/0

Eyes: Monofilament

Tail: Olive grizzly hackle fluff

Rib: Clear 4X monofilament

Back: Clear plastic or Scudback across the entire top of the fly

Abdomen: Olive-brown Scintilla
Legs: Soft olive grizzly hackle fibers
Thorax: Olive-brown Scintilla, picked out

KAUFMANN'S LAKE DRAGON
Hook: Sizes 6 to 10, 3X long
Thread: Olive, 6/0
Eyes: Monofilament
Tail: Olive grizzly marabou, short
Rib: Fine copper wire
Abdomen: 50 percent olive rabbit then blue, purple, green, amber, olive, rust, and brown angora goat
Legs: Olive ringneck rump
Wingcase: Brown turkey quill
Thorax: [repeat]

BEAVERPELT
Hook: Sizes 2 to 8, 2X to 3X long
Thread: Tan, 3/0
UnderBody: Build up the body taper with floss or small wool to conserve dubbing
Body: Brownish gray beaver or a blend of beaver and red fox, dubbed thickly with tapers on both ends
Hackle: Long black pheasant rump or black hen

SPARROW
Hook: Sizes 6 to 10, 2X to 3X long
Thread: Black, 3/0 to 6/0
Tail: Dyed black pheasant rump
Abdomen: Arizona Synthetic Peacock, tied in thick past the mid-point of the hook shank
Hackle: Dyed black pheasant rump

Head: Two black-dyed pheasant aftershafts wound around the thread to form chenille

JR'S 'POSSUM BUG
This is my version of the Dolls Hair
Hook: Sizes 6 to 10, 2X to 3X long
Thread: Black or brown, 3/0
Abdomen: Large oval body, dubbed with Arizona Crystal 'Possum (your color of choice) halfway up
Hook Shank: Build up body with floss or small wool to conserve dubbing
Hackle: Soft natural brown hen hackle
Thorax: Same as abdomen, dubbed smaller

GIERACH DRAGON
Hook: Tiemco 200R, sizes 6 to 10
Thread: Black, 6/0
Rib: Fine flat gold tinsel
Body: Hare's ear dubbing
Underwing: Dyed dark brown deer hair, tied inverted
Wing: Dark turkey tail, short
Legs: Ringneck pheasant flank fibers
Eyes: Monofilament
Head: Hare's ear dubbing

DREDGE BUG
Hook: Sizes 6 to 10, 2X long nymph
Tail: Pheasant rump
Body: Build up the body with floss or small wool over half the hook shank. Dub over with Arizona Simi Seal of your preferred color.

Rib: Copper wire
Hackle: Hen or dyed pheasant rump of your desired color
Head: Same as the body, only smaller

Nymphs and Scuds

These patterns can be weighted or have beadheads.

HARE'S EAR

Hook: Sizes 12 to 20, standard or 1X long nymph
Thread: Tan, 6/0
Tail: Small clump of hare's mask or a pinch of brown soft hackle
Rib: Flat gold Mylar tinsel (optional)
Abdomen: Hare's ear dubbing in natural, olive, or black
Wingcase: Turkey treated with Flexament, or pearl Saltwater Flashabou
Thorax: Hare's Ear dubbed thick and picked out
Legs: Optional—brown soft hen hackle or brown partridge

PHEASANT TAIL

Hook: Sizes 12 to 20, standard or 1X long nymph
Thread: Tobacco brown Danville, 6/0
Tail: Tips of six ringneck pheasant tail fibers
Rib: Fine copper wire
Wingcase: Turkey treated with Flexament, or pearl Saltwater Flashabou
Thorax: Arizona Synthetic Peacock, natural
Legs: Butt ends of pheasant tail

fibers trimmed to the end of the thorax

PHEASANT TAIL SOFT-HACKLE

This is a good emerger pattern
Hook: Sizes 121 to 20, standard or 1X long nymph
Thread: Tobacco brown Danville, 6/0
Tail: Tips of ringneck pheasant tail fibers
Rib: Fine copper wire
Thorax: Arizona Synthetic Peacock, natural
Hackle: Brown partridge

JR'S MAYFLY

Hook: Tiemco 2487, sizes 14 to 22
Thread: Color to match body; 8/0
Tail: Three strands of pheasant rump or partridge
Abdomen: Arizona Micro Sheen, to match the naturals (olive or brown tones)
Rib: Fine copper or gold wire
Shellback and Wingcase: Fine olive or gold holographic tinsel on top of the entire body
Thorax: Arizona Synthetic Peacock, color to match body

FOAM CALLIBAETIS EMERGER

This excellent emerger pattern is from Philip Rowley of British Columbia
Hook: Tiemco 2487, sizes 10 to 16
Thread: Tan or olive, 8/0
Tail: Micro Fleck turkey flats, partridge, or wood duck. Fan three fibers over a ball of thread at the end of the hook.

Rib: Pearl Krystal Flash, one strand counterwound over the body

Body: *Callibaetis* tan or olive Superfine dubbing

Wing: Gray poly yarn

Wingcase: Narrow strip of gray closed-cell foam

Legs: Grizzly saddle palmered over thorax

Thorax: *Callibaetis* tan or olive Superfine dubbing

ZUG BUG

Hook: Sizes 10 to 20, standard or 1X long nymph

Thread: Black, 8/0 or 6/0

Tail: Three peacock sword tips

Rib: Silver or gold Mylar tinsel

Body: Arizona Synthetic Peacock, natural

Wing Pad: Mallard or mallard-dyed wood duck

Hackle: Brown hen, tied beard-style or wet-fly-style

PRINCE NYMPH

Hook: Sizes 10 to 14, 2X or 3X long

Thread: Black, 6/0 or 8/0

Tail: Brown goose biots

Rib: Silver Mylar tinsel

Body: Arizona Synthetic Peacock, natural

Horns: White goose biots

Hackle: Brown hen, tied beard-style or wet-fly-style

PEACOCK LADY

Hook: Sizes 8 to 12, 2X to 3X long

Thread: Brown, 6/0

Tail: Red golden pheasant tippets

Rear Hackle: Two wraps of grizzly saddle

Body: Peacock counterwound around thread or natural Arizona Synthetic Peacock

Front Hackle: Two wraps of brown saddle

SUNRISE SPECIAL

Hook: Sizes 4 to 10, 2X to 3X long

Thread: Brown, 6/0

Tail: Red golden pheasant tippets

Rib: Flat gold Mylar tinsel

Hackle: Brown saddle, palmered up the body between tinsel wraps

KILLER

Hook: Sizes 8 to 14, 2X long

Thread: Brown, 6/0

Tail: Brown marabou, tied the same length as the body

Rib: Flat gold Mylar tinsel

Body: Peacock herl counterwound around thread or natural Arizona Synthetic Peacock

HALFBACK

Hook: Sizes 12 to 16, standard or 1X long nymph

Thread: Brown, 6/0

Tail: Pheasant tailfibers

Body: Arizona Synthetic Peacock, natural

Wingcase: Pheasant tail fibers

Hackle: Brown saddle palmered through the thorax

Thorax: Natural Arizona Synthetic Peacock, tied larger than the abdomen

TIMBERLINE
Hook: Sizes 16 to 20, 1X long nymph
Thread: Tan, 6/0
Tail: Ringneck pheasant tail fibers
Rib: Fine copper wire
Body: Hare's ear
Wingcase: Ringneck pheasant tail fibers
Thorax: Hare's ear
Legs: Ringneck pheasant tail fibers, tips from wingcase

JR'S SCUDBACK
Hook: Tiemco 2487, sizes 16 to 20
Thread: Color to match body, 6/0 or 8/0
Tail: Small pinch of Arizona Scud Blend in assorted colors
Shellback: Clear or gray ⅛-inch Scudback
Rib: Clear 6X tippet material
Body: Arizona Scud Blend (color of your choice), teased with Velcro underneath to imitate legs
Tying note: Usually tied small in grayish tones to imitate the *Hyalella* scud

SCUDLY
This is Larry Allen's Lee's Ferry scud pattern
Hook: Standard or 1X long nymph hook
Thread: Color to match body, 6/0
Abdomen: Arizona Scud Blend, color of your choice
Rib: Gold or copper flat Mylar tinsel
Hackle: Partridge

Thorax: Arizona Scud Blend, dubbed thicker than the abdomen and slightly teased with Velcro
Tying note: I like to add a copper or old beadhead

WD-40
Hook: Tiemco 2487, sizes 18 to 20
Thread: Olive Danville, 6/0
Tail: Wood duck or mallard-dyed wood duck
Body: Olive Danville, 6/0
Rib: Optional—gold wire
Wingcase: Butts of wood duck or mallard flank
Thorax: Olive-gray dubbing
Tying note: Sometimes I put a tiny, clear glass bead in front

Midges

DISCO MIDGE
Hook: Tiemco 2487, sizes 18 to 22
Thread: Black, 8/0
Body: Pearl Krystal Flash
Thorax: Arizona Synthetic Peacock, natural

ULTRA MIDGE
Hook: Tiemco 2487, sizes 18 to 22
Thread: Assorted
Body: Three or four strands of Ultra Hair. The body can take on a segmented effect if you use two or three darker colors and one lighter color. Using light-colored thread underneath will show better segmentation.

Thorax: Arizona Synthetic Peacock, color to match the naturals

Tying notes: This very durable, effective midge can be tied in a wide variety of colors to match the naturals. It's sometimes tied with a tiny, clear glass bead in front.

SRI CDC EMERGER

Hook: Tiemco 2487, sizes 18 to 20

Thread: Olive, 8/0

Tail: Three iridescent olive-gray fibers from ringneck pheasant back

Rib: Pearl Krystal Flash

Abdomen: Olive Arizona Micro Sheen (or color to match the naturals)

Wingcase: Light dun or white CDC, looped

Thorax: Arizona Synthetic Peacock, light

12

A Final Look

Between the two of us, we've fished a large majority of the trout waters from the East Coast to the West. And of all the states we've fished, Arizona has to be the most sensitive to the forces of both man and nature. Trout fishing in the high desert is so dependent on snowfall and the whims and fancies of humans that it's extremely difficult to predict its future. Sometimes it's hard to recognize which is the bigger problem—Mother Nature or the laws with which we govern our fishing waters. We can't do much about the amounts of precipitation, of course, but with the laws we do have something to say.

First, let's look at the physical outlook of our streams and lakes. After 4 years of mild drought conditions in Arizona, Mother Nature relinquished her stranglehold in 1998 and sent us El Niño. Although this weather occurrence affected many of the western states in an adverse way, it was a blessing to us. Snowpack in the mountains was above average, which meant abundant fresh water for lakes and streams in spring. As this book goes to press in the summer of 1998, we're expecting the streams to run all through the season, meaning healthy, holdover fish for more natural reproduction. Lakes will be stocked with large amounts of trout and have a better chance of survival next winter, with more water available.

One or maybe two of our high lakes suffered some degree of winterkill in 1998, if not total. This was from low water levels prior to freezeup and tremendous amounts of weed growth. Still, the last time Sunrise Lake winterkilled, the White Mountain Game and Fish Department loaded it with huge amounts of trout to replenish the stocks, and we expect the same to occur this year, if needed.

We've heard recent reports of as much as 5 feet of water going over the spillway at Chevelon Canyon Lake. Some of our desert lakes are above the high-water mark; Oak Creek and the Verde River are flowing high. Lee's Ferry is fishing as well as it ever has and Lake Powell is stable, with no threat of flooding or drought in the near future. All in all, it looks like 1998 will be a good year for fishing, with ample water for all species of fish from the high trout lakes to the desert bass lakes.

Now let's look at the bureaucratic side of our fishing. Both the White Mountain and San Carlos Indian tribes are heading in positive directions. The White Mountain tribe is looking into creating more quality fisheries, maintaining some for the fisherman who'd like to catch that wallmount and others as traditional put-and-take lakes, where the family can go and get a stringer for dinner. This is good management, in our view. We believe in catch-and-release fishing, but we don't expect everyone else to share our views, and we can appreciate a fresh trout dinner as well as the next person. What we don't advocate is catching your limit and going home to put the fish in the freezer to be fed to the cat two years later . . . that makes no sense to us. Trout are too valuable to waste and in most cases, too much fun to catch just once. Throw them back to grow and do it again, and again, and again.

The White Mountain Apaches have even designated two lakes as catch-and-release, Earl Park in 1996 and Pacheta in 1997. Earl Park has lately grown some big browns, and had some of the hardest-fighting rainbows on the hill. The Apaches have wintered well here; we caught several in spring 1997 that were in the upper end spawning. They were bright pink all over. We've never seen prettier trout, and they fought hard as well.

As far as the state waters are concerned, there is mixed opinion. The waters handled by the Arizona Game and Fish Department have always been maintained for the majority of the fishermen in the state, which of course are not fly-fishermen. This was acceptable in years past when there was not such a conscientious effort to maintain a quality environment. Attitudes today are very different, however. Kids are taught to appreciate even the smallest bluegill, and they know that if they handle a fish carefully and return it to the water, they can come back tomorrow and enjoy it again. I think we can credit some of this awareness to the state's bass clubs and their tournaments, which give the fish the respect they deserve. We hope that someday Arizona Game and Fish will recognize the growing desire for quality fishing and maintain some waters around the state for that purpose. We think such waters would be well received and used by all.

RECOMMENDATIONS

Arizona trout fishing needs help. For the state's streams and lakes to continue as a recreational resource into the new millennium, and for more people to enjoy the thrills of fishing in general and fly-fishing in particular, some changes must occur, based on a recognition that many streams in the state can't hold trout year-round. Here, then, are some of our recommendations.

Support a Diversity of Trout Species

Locals say that some of the best trout streams, especially those in the Springerville-Alpine area, are no longer stocked with trout because of the spinedace minnow. The Little Colorado River in the Springerville area used to hold trout. It no longer does. Eagle Creek south of Alpine received planted trout until a few years ago and the same goes for the Blue River. Some people are concerned that trout will eat this small, endangered minnow. But anglers—the ones who contribute money to the coffers of Game and Fish—want to fish for trout.

So the Game and Fish Department is caught in the middle. On one side they have the environmentalists who want to restore native fish to Arizona streams and rivers. On the other side they have anglers who want to catch trout. One of Arizona's problems is that rainbow and brown trout are not native to the state, so some environmentalists want to see them eradicated, or at least decreased.

Imagine what would happen in the East if authorities wanted to kill the browns and rainbows and revert to the region's only native trout, the brookie. It's a ridiculous thought, isn't it? In Arizona some want to restore streams to Apache trout only. Yet in many streams rainbows and browns have thrived. Why sacrifice these latter two species to restore a native fish?

Expand the Winter Stocking Program

When the Arizona Game and Fish Department began stocking the Salt River below Saguaro Lake during the winter, hundreds of anglers—both bait- and fly-fishers—crowded this new recreational resource. Recently, however, the flow on the Salt River has been so reduced as to eliminate any quality fishing. Game and Fish is at the mercy of the Salt River Project. Who knows if this problem will ever be resolved? Yet many winter and permanent residents enjoyed the winter fishing.

Why doesn't Game and Fish look at other streams and rivers that have the potential for winter fly-fishing? We believe the following streams offer possibilities for winter stocking:

Tonto Creek flows from the Mogollon Rim and enters Roosevelt Lake

50 miles above Phoenix. If you travel north along AZ 188 from Roosevelt Lake in the Tonto Basin you'll see Tonto Creek flowing within half a mile of the road. Here Tonto would be fishable all winter, easily accessible, and close to a heavy concentration of anglers. And there's at least 10 miles of water to fish. A study conducted by the Arizona Department of Environmental Quality found that this section of the stream holds a fantastic trico hatch from March through November. What great matching-the-hatch opportunities this would bring. What would happen to the trout in spring when Tonto Creek warms? They might migrate downstream to the lake or find cool springs or tributaries. Certainly they'd have a better chance to survive the hot weather than those trout stocked in urban lakes.

Cherry Creek flows about 35 miles east of Tonto Creek. It begins near Young and flows south into the Salt River. Temperatures in its lower end are also moderate during the winter. This, too, could be stocked.

For years we fished the Verde River on the Fort McDowell Indian Reservation. Recently tribal authorities closed the river to fishing. Why not stock the river from below Bartlett Reservoir down to the reservation? Again, this section would provide fly-fishing all winter long.

Increase the Number of Trout Waters with Special Regulations

The regulations on most Arizona trout waters are catch and kill—anglers come to catch their limit. What would happen if limits were reduced? The Apache Indian Reservation has done this—and much more toward the conservation of trout. They're to be commended for their efforts.

Enhance the Tailwaters

Tailwaters offer several advantages to anglers. First, they can equalize a stream's water flow throughout the year; second, because they draw water from the bottom of a lake, they cool the river below. Arizona has two tailwaters. Everyone knows how productive the Colorado River has become—but few realize the potential for the Salt River below Saguaro Lake, if only its flows were steady. See chapter 3 for more discussion of the Salt.

Get Involved

Only in numbers can fly-fishers have an effect on the future of the Salt River or the dozens of issues presently upsetting the qualtity of Arizona's fly-fishing. How can you get involved? Support the worthwhile Trout Unlimited and Federation of Fly Fishers clubs in the state. Contact the one nearest your home, or the national headquarters. The Resources section of this book provides additional information on regional organizations and fly shops.

RESOURCES

National and Regional Organizations

FEDERATION OF FLY FISHERS (FFF)
Eastern Rocky Mountain Council
Director: Carmine Isgro
President: Dan Turner
National Headquarters
PO Box 1595
Bozeman, MT 59771
(406) 585-7592

TROUT UNLIMITED (TU)

Old Pueblo Chapter
Membership Info:
3542 West Amber Terrace
Tucson, AZ 85741
Wendy Hanvold: (520) 355-2261
Meetings: first Wednesday of each month at 7:30 PM
El Parador Restaurant
2744 East Broadway Boulevard

Zane Grey Chapter
4730 North 7th Avenue
Phoenix, AZ 85013
President: Jerry Jenkins
Membership Info:
1907 South Don Luis Circle

Mesa, AZ 85202
Gary L. Walsh: (602) 838-5732
GWalsh7797@aol.com

National Headquarters
800 Follin Lane, Suite 250
Vienna, VA 22180-4906

ARIZONA FLYCASTERS
PO Box 44976
Phoenix, AZ 85064
President: Mike Costello
Vice President: Carmine Isgro
(602) 972-3461
Secretary: Ed Yanez (602) 878-2002
Treasurer: Steve Stevens (602) 494-9949
Meetings: second Thursday of each month at 6:30 PM
Sunnyslope Community Center

DAME JULIANA ANGLERS
PO Box 1727
Phoenix, AZ 85001-1727
Contact: juliana@azoutbackanglers.com
Offers women's seminars with women instructors, outings for women only, conservation projects, and other great activities.

DESERT FLYCASTERS CLUB
PO Box 41271
Mesa, AZ, 85274-1271
Contact: Ted Miskinnis
Meetings: second Wednesday of
    each month at 7 PM
VFW, 65 South McDonald (at
    Main Street)

NORTHERN ARIZONA FLYCASTERS
PO Box 2924
Flagstaff, AZ 86003
Contact: John Marvin (520) 774-
    8380 (H), (520) 779-4395 (W)
Meetings: first Thursday of each
    month at 7 PM
Shepherd of the Hills Lutheran
    Church
1601 North San Francisco Street

Arizona's Fly Shops

Cottonwood

WAGER'S FLY SHOP
1 South Main Street
Cottonwood, AZ 86326
(520) 639-2022

Flagstaff

BABBITT'S
15 East Aspen Avenue
Flagstaff, AZ 86001
(520) 779-3253

PEACE SURPLUS
14 West Route 66
Flagstaff, AZ 86001
(520) 779-4521

Greer

X-DIAMOND RANCH
Box 791
Springerville, AZ 85938
(520) 333-2286

Phoenix

CANYON CREEK ANGLERS
21 West Camelback Road
Phoenix, AZ 85012
(602) 277-8195

ALTA VISTA ANGLERS
4730 North 7th Avenue
Phoenix, AZ 85013
(602) 277-3111

ELLINGTON'S HAND-TIED FLIES
3814 East Oak Street
Phoenix, AZ 85008
(602) 244-1803

Pinetop

SKIER'S EDGE
PO Box 1129 D
Pinetop, AZ
(520) 676-2000

Prescott

LYNX CREEK UNLIMITED
130 West Gurley Street, Suite 307
Prescott, AZ 86301
(520) 776-7088

Scottsdale

GLENN TINNIN'S COMPLEAT FLYFISHING
10050 North Scottsdale Road
Scottsdale, AZ 85254
(602) 368-9280

4J's TROUTFITTERS
10869 North Scottsdale Road
Scottsdale, AZ 85254
(602) 905-1400

Tempe

ARIZONA FLYFISHING
31 West Baseline Road
Tempe, AZ 85283
(602) 730-6808

Tucson

TIGHT LINES
4444 East Grant Road, Suite 113
Tucson, AZ 85712
(520) 322-9444

INDEX

201

Also from The Countryman Press and Backcountry Guides

Backcountry Guides

Fishing Vermont's Streams and Lakes
Great Lakes Steelhead: A Guided Tour for Fly-Anglers
Michigan Trout Streams
Mid-Atlantic Trout Streams and Their Hatches
Pennsylvania Trout Streams and Their Hatches
Tailwater Trout in the South
Trout Streams of Southern Appalachia
Virginia Trout Streams
Wisconsin and Minnesota Trout Streams

Bass Flies
Building Classic Salmon Flies
Fishing Small Streams with a Fly Rod
Flies in the Water, Fish in the Air
Fly-Fishing with Children: A Guide for Parents
Fly-Tying Tips
Fundamentals of Building a Bamboo Fly-Rod
The Golden Age of Fly-Fishing: The Best of The Sportsman, 1927–1937
Good Fishing in the Adirondacks
Good Fishing in the Catskills
Good Fishing in Lake Ontario and Its Tributaries
Good Fishing in Western New York
Ice Fishing: A Complete Guide...Basic to Advanced
Ultralight Spin-Fishing
Universal Fly Tying Guide

We offer many more books on hiking, biking, travel, nature, and other subjects. Our books are available at bookstores and outdoor stores everywhere. For more information or a free catalog, please call 1-800-245-4151 or write to us at The Countryman Press, PO Box 748, Woodstock, Vermont 05091. You can find us on the Internet at www.countrymanpress.com.